AF473808

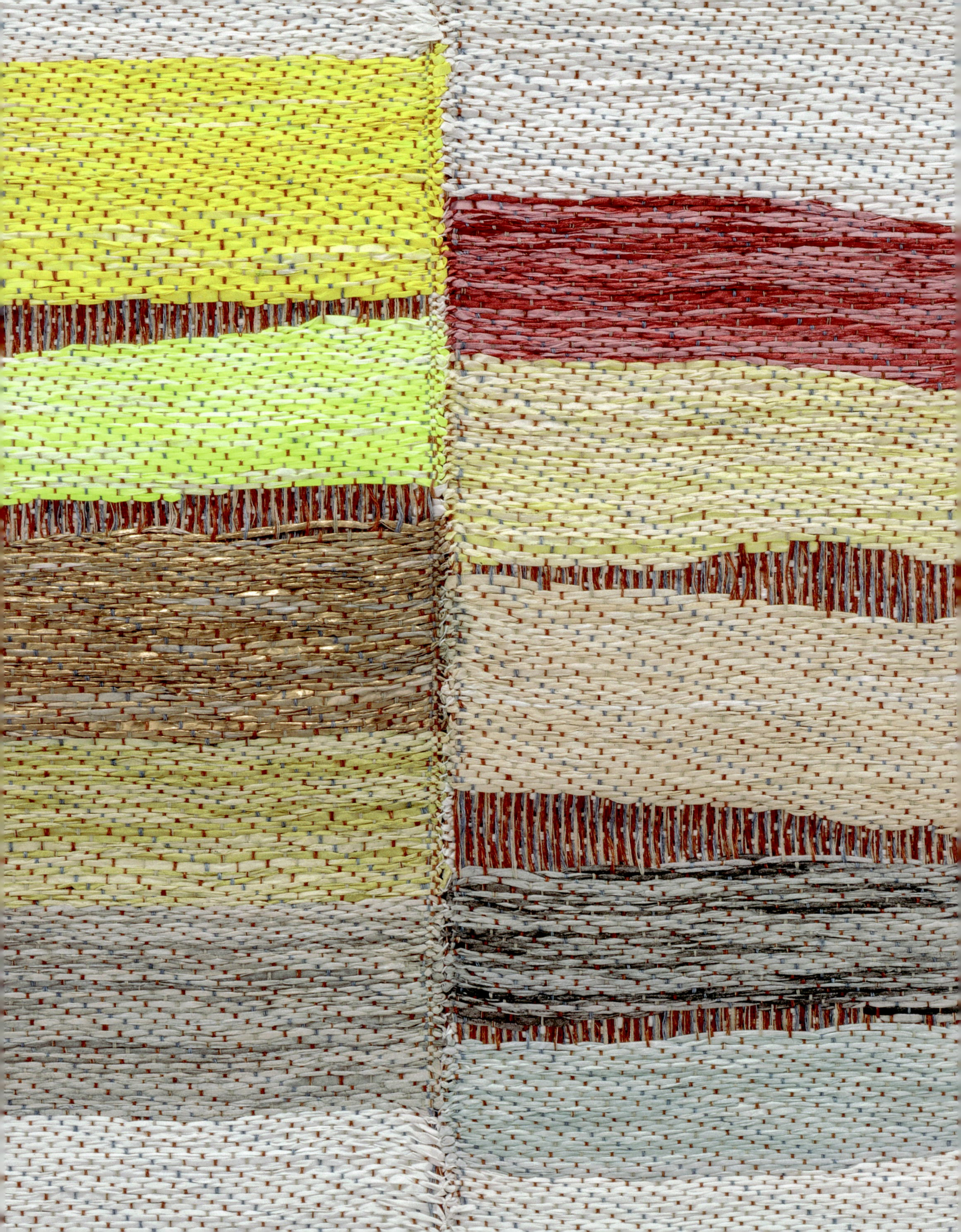

Currents 38

Christy Matson

Edited by Monica Obniski

with a contribution by Su Wu and a conversation with the artist

Milwaukee Art Museum

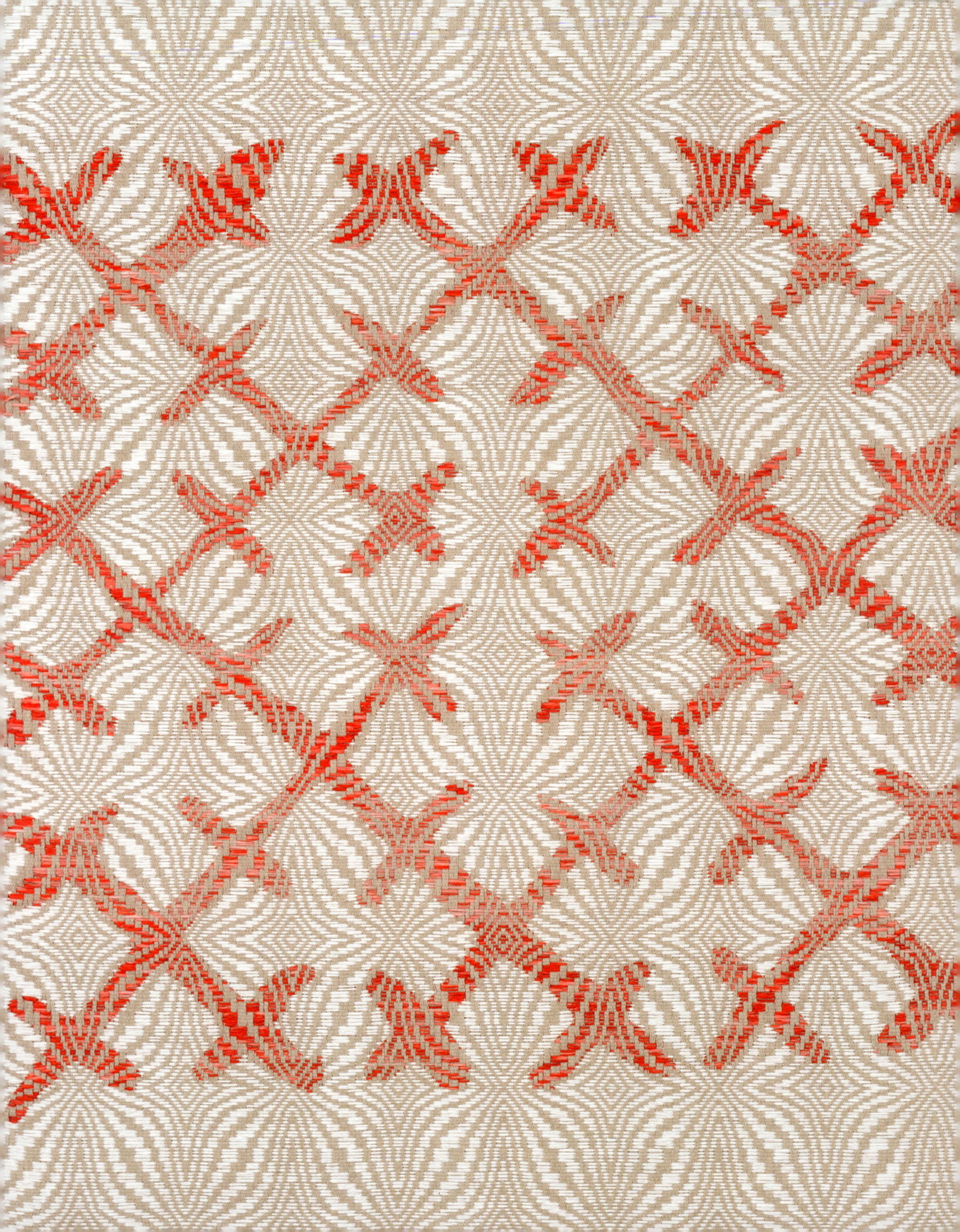

Contents

Director's Foreword

The Milwaukee Art Museum debuted its *Currents* exhibition series in 1982 with the work of Cynthia Carlson, a key figure of New York's Pattern and Decoration movement. The series provides artists who are creating compelling work the platform of an exhibition to debut new art to our audience. With *Currents 38*, the Museum is proud to present the work of Christy Matson.

This exhibition was set to open in 2020, a fitting year to celebrate the work of a woman, as it was the centennial of the Nineteeth Amendment. That it will open in 2022, following the upheaval of the global pandemic, demonstrates the Museum's fortitude and its commitment to the artist. Matson has helped expand the conversation around textiles as contemporary art through weavings that collapse the artificial boundaries between fine art and textiles. Art writer Su Wu has eloquently noted in this volume that Matson's works "interrogate the medium of textile itself, gleefully and irreverently dipping into its associations."

This is the first *Currents* exhibition to feature textiles. Monica Obniski, former Demmer Curator of 20th- and 21st-Century Design, championed Matson for the series, and the Museum has the opportunity to share and support the work of this exciting artist thanks to Obniski's astute eye and hard work. Christy Matson was an enthusiastic collaborator, and we are grateful for her active involvement. Additionally, Sam Vinz and Claire Warner of Volume Gallery, Chicago, deserve special recognition for their assistance. Exhibitions such as *Currents 38: Christy Matson* cannot happen without the lenders who generously share works from their collections. We extend our thanks to the museums and many private collectors that made it possible for such a broad representation of Matson's work to be brought together for this project. Finally, we thank the Center for Craft, Asheville, North Carolina, for a Craft Research Fund Exhibition Grant in support of this meaningful exhibition.

Marcelle Polednik, PhD
Donna and Donald Baumgartner Director
Milwaukee Art Museum

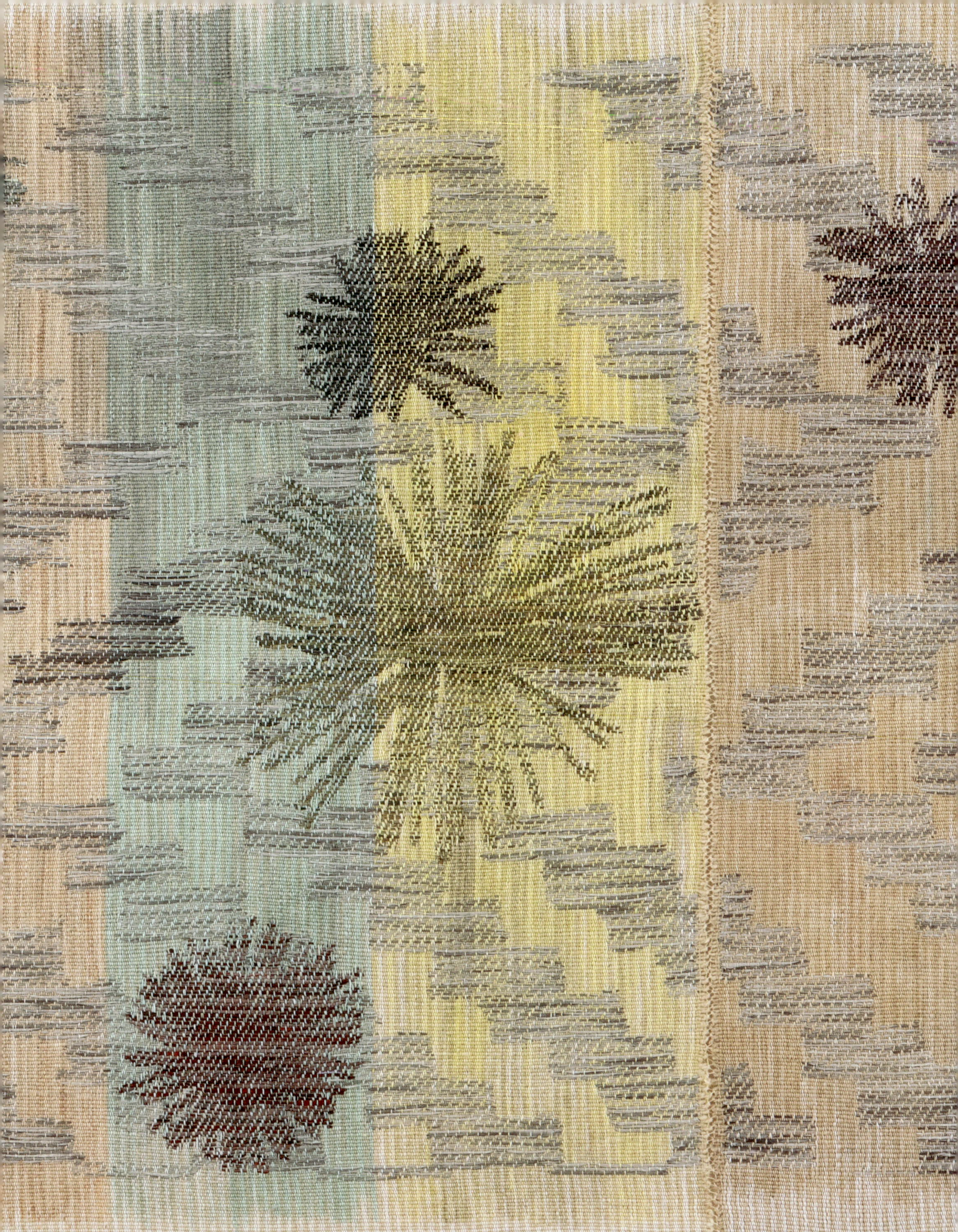

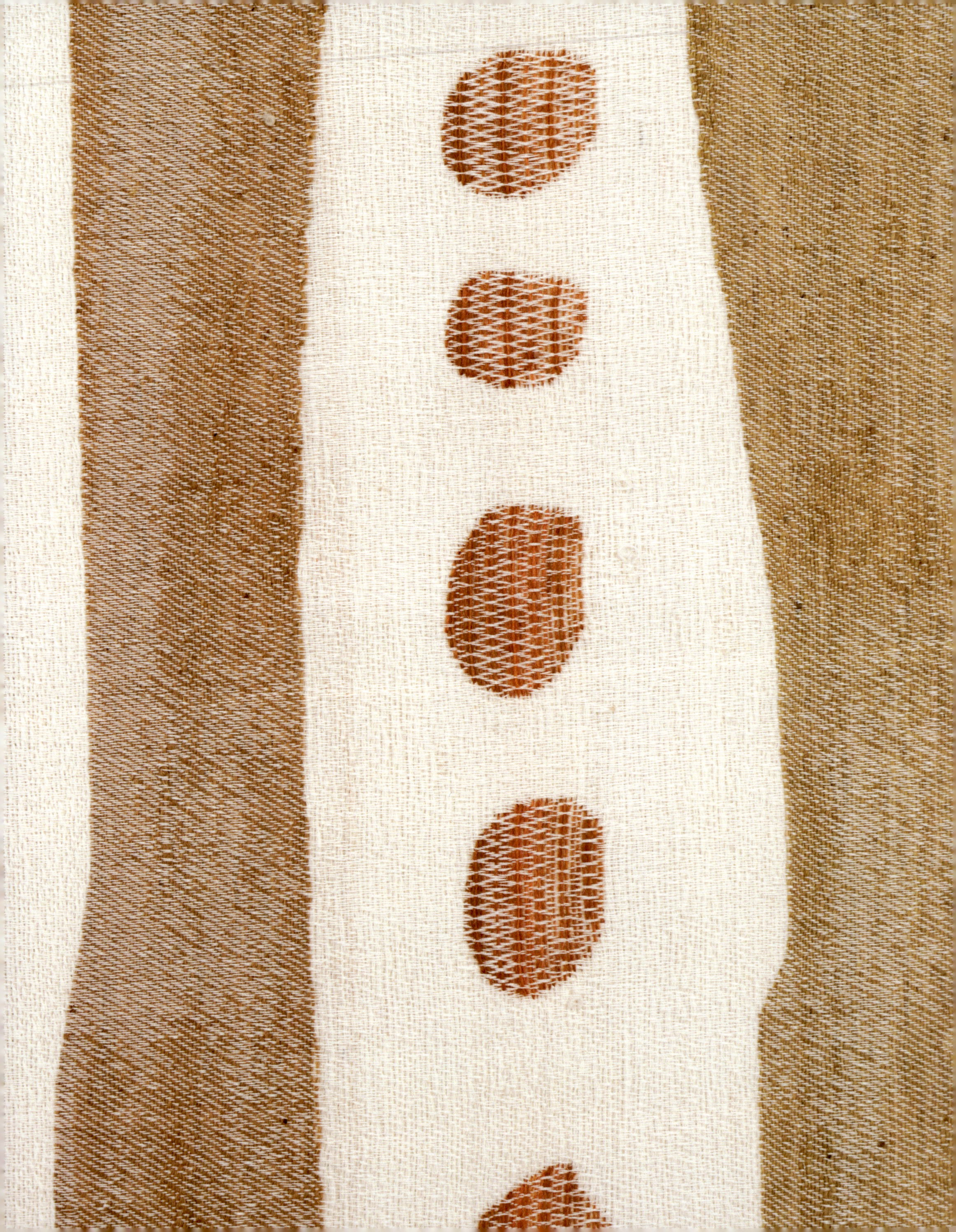

Acknowledgments

The Milwaukee Art Museum is honored to work with the Los Angeles–based artist Christy Matson on the thirty-eighth iteration of the *Currents* series. The exciting work that she is creating is part of a craft renaissance within contemporary art. My sincerest thanks go to Christy, who has been the consummate collaborator. It has been a great pleasure to work with you on this journey that has inspired close looking and deep thinking.

Some of the most steadfast supporters of Christy's work are the lenders to this exhibition. From the Art Institute of Chicago, I'd like to thank Melinda Watt and Erica Warren, and from the Los Angeles County Museum of Art, Bobbye Tigerman, for being generous—in spirit and with loans—curatorial colleagues. There are several individuals who have graciously parted with their weavings for the duration of this show: McArthur Binion, Heiji and Brian Black, Jennifer and Dan Gilbert, Lisa and Philip Kepler, Teresa Manns, Kelly Padden and Mathias Kessler, Gabrielle and Nick Sainati, Monica Schaffer, Lizzy and Josh Scheinfeld, Cecilia and Ira Wolfson, Margo Wolowiec, and others who wish to remain anonymous. Thanks also to Rebecca Camacho Presents, San Francisco, and Timothy Taylor Gallery, London and New York. Chicago's Volume Gallery, founded by Sam Vinz and Claire Warner, has been a remarkable partner in this endeavor. I am extremely grateful to Sam and Claire for their fellowship.

Working with the staff of the Milwaukee Art Museum on *Currents 38: Christy Matson* has been a rewarding experience. I am deeply appreciative of Donna and Donald Baumgartner Director Marcelle Polednik, PhD, and Margaret Andera, interim chief curator and curator of contemporary art, for championing this project. Many remarkable colleagues have been instrumental in this endeavor, including Chyna Bounds, Liz Flaig, and aryn kresol in Curatorial; Lydelle Abbott Janes in Registration; David Russick in Exhibition Design; Abby Ashley and Therese Palazzari in Development; Terri White in Conservation; and the preparators led by Arthur Mohagen III.

The exhibition publication has been expertly managed by Lucia | Marquand and editor Tanya Heinrich. Su Wu also deserves praise for enhancing the catalog with her thoughtful and poetic essay.

Christy Matson would like to extend a note of immense gratitude to Sam Vinz and Claire Warner of Volume Gallery for their infinite generosity, dedication, and support of this exhibition. None of this would have been possible without their commitment to her practice.

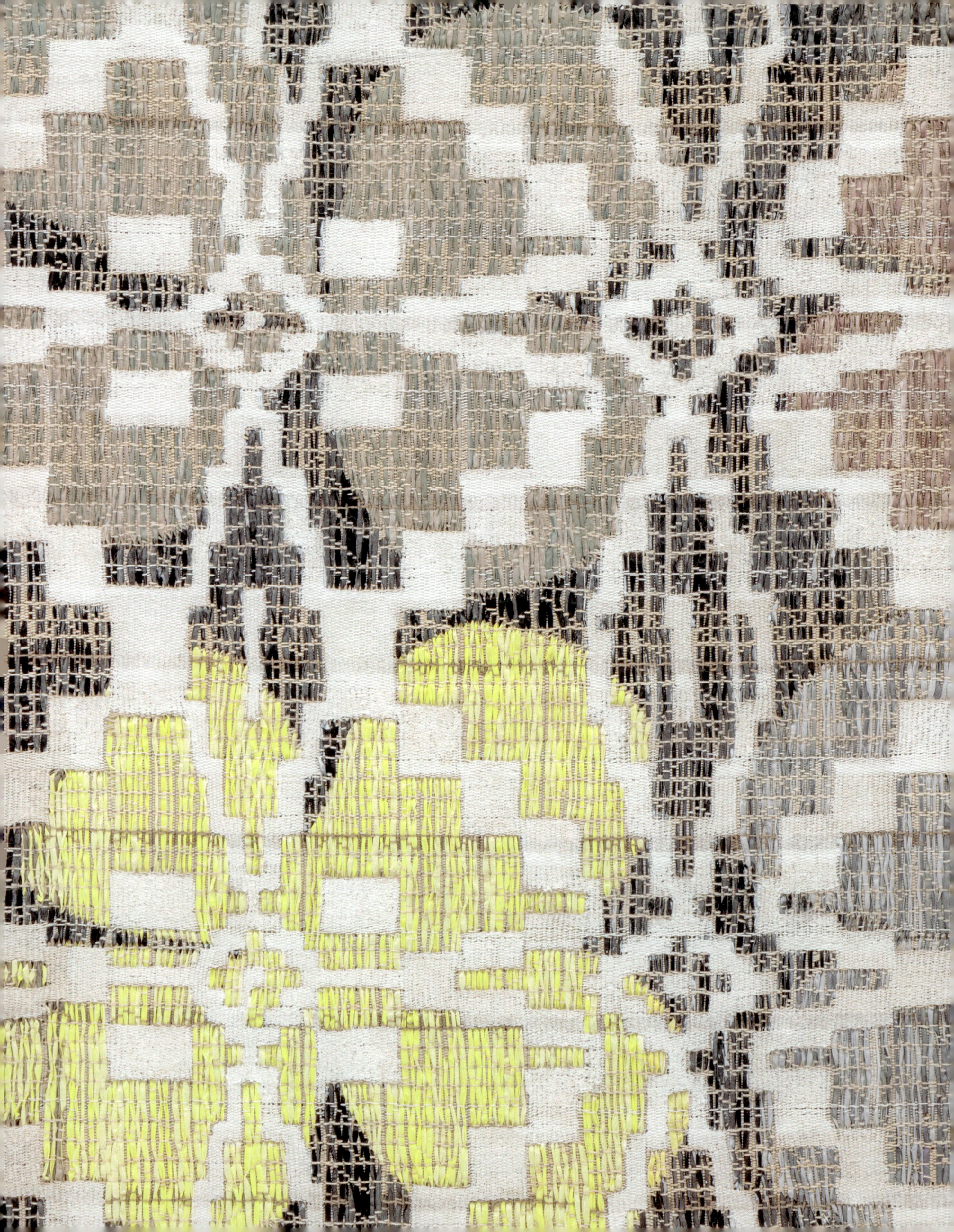

Surface and Depth: The Woven Pictures of Christy Matson

Monica Obniski

“Usefulness does not prevent a thing, anything, from being art,” noted the German-born American artist-designer Anni Albers, who argued that thoughtfulness, care, and sensitivity, as they relate to form, elevate objects into the realm of art.[1] This essay will not debate the merits of incorporating textiles into the canon of contemporary art—that work is currently being undertaken by many—but instead acknowledges that this medium, long associated with the decorative arts, has been embraced by the broader art world.[2] More than fifty years ago, the Museum of Modern Art’s groundbreaking show *Wall Hangings* (1969, curated by Mildred Constantine and Jack Lenor Larsen) was the first group exhibition to display contemporary woven work within the context of contemporary art, and today, the boundaries between media have destabilized to a point of inclusivity. It’s about time.

Textiles, as a field of cultural production, are also a system of language, full of meaning, and thus a form of communication. In fact, artist Beryl Korot calls the loom “one of the most ancient of communications technologies.”[3] Within this field, weaving has a long history, and the work of Los Angeles–based artist Christy Matson may be located within this tradition as part of a new craft revival. Matson creates woven pictures that participate in minimalism, abstraction, and decoration—languages shared with painting. But Matson also constructs a unique pictorial language to communicate within the system of textiles. Because she often crafts objects in series, works such as *Synecdoche* and *Synecdoche II* (pages 12 and 13) introduce the idea of woven pictures that are meant to be seen and understood together. As a pair, these wall

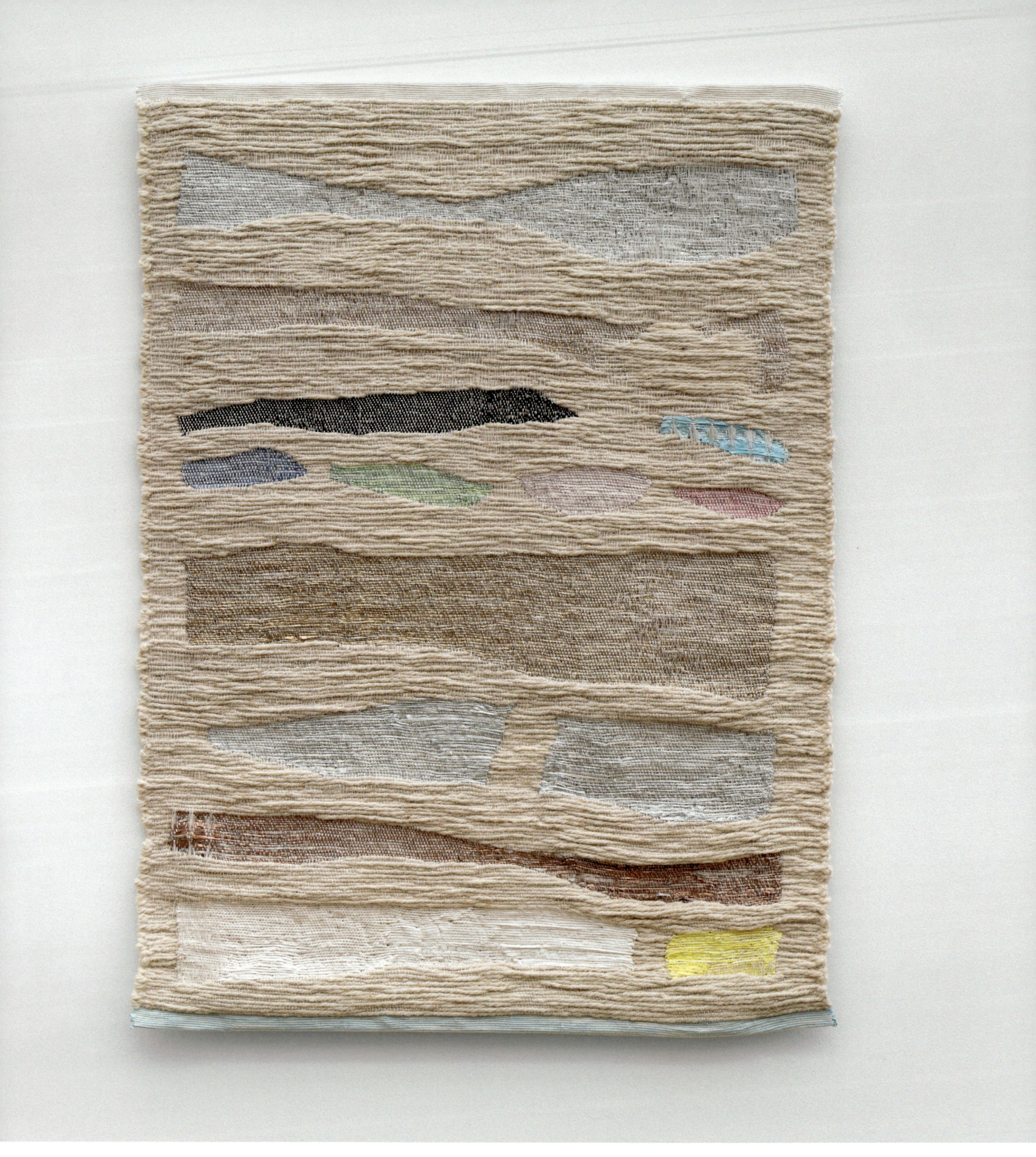

Synecdoche, 2018

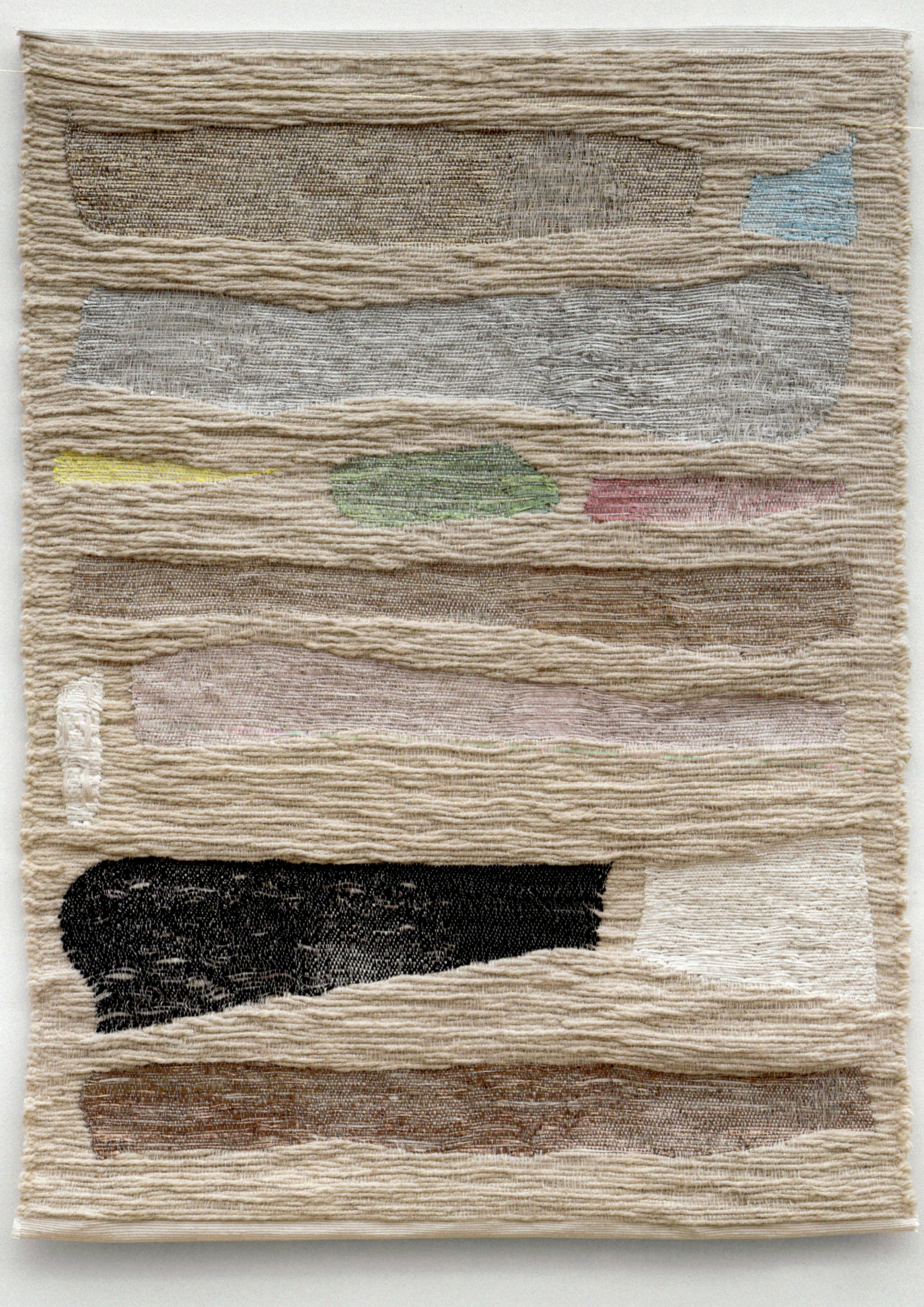

Synecdoche II, 2018

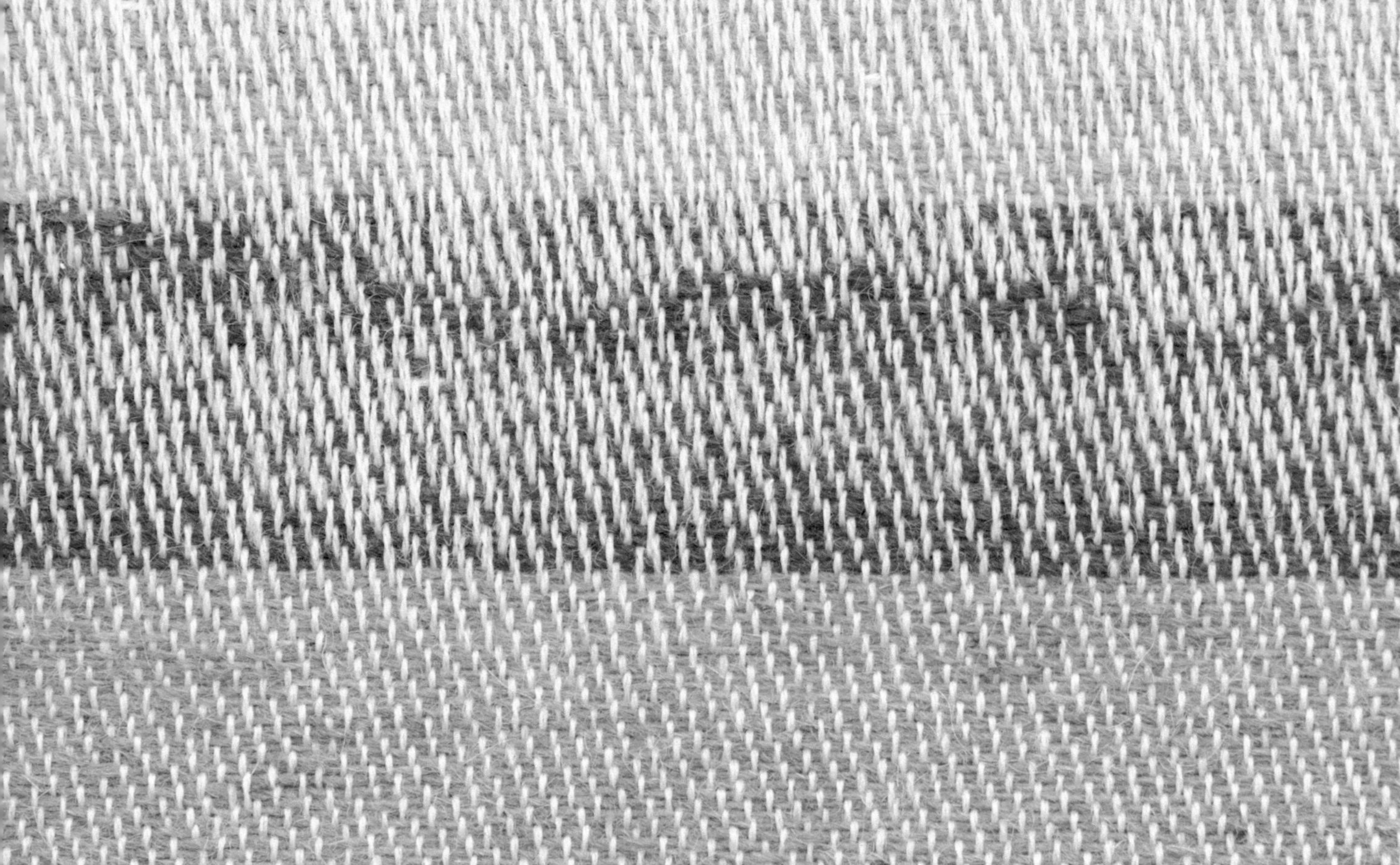

Fig. 1 Christy Matson, *Untitled (Shapes and Figures)*, 2018. Acrylic and spray paint on paper, wool, and cotton, 56 × 43 in. Private collection

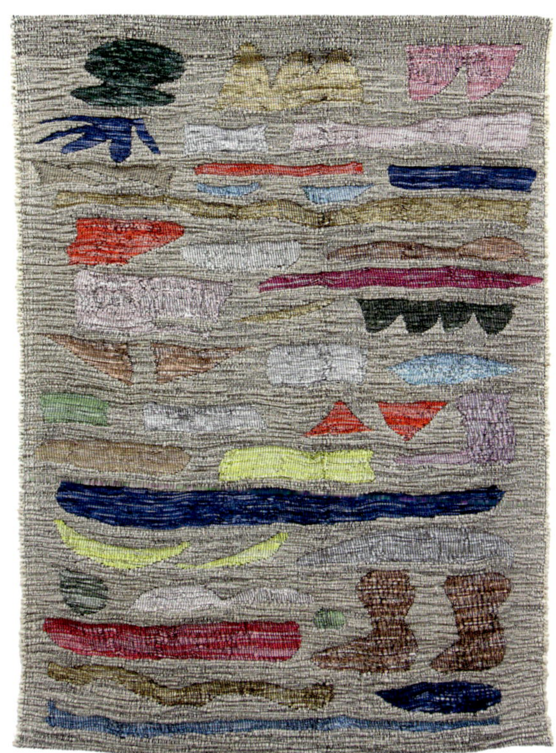

hangings begin to resemble two pages of a novel, in which the woven fields of color might stand in for words on a page. True to its title, *Synecdoche*'s colorful interludes contain the parts that can represent the whole. In a different but similarly composed work, *Untitled (Shapes and Figures)* (fig. 1), woven while Matson was a visiting artist at the University of Wisconsin–Madison in 2018, reveals various shapes that can function as hieroglyphics or pictograms, in which the blue rectangles might reference water or sky and the yellow curved elements can intimate bananas. Matson's pictorial language is composed of cyphers and shapes that transcend time and place to create a universal textile language.

Matson's woven pictures may seem like a contradiction in terms: pictures, as evocative as flat paintings hung on a wall (and therefore referencing tropes of contemporary art), that are woven—as textiles are her medium. Matson thinks of herself as a painter in the broadest sense of the word, making marks on her canvas of choice, and identifies Helen Frankenthaler as one of her influences (fig. 13). The aura of this color field painter appears in Matson's minimalist works, particularly from her 2016 *Haptic* series, such as *Hershey* (facing page). Painterly effects are rendered with yarns of varying textures at differing intervals to create subtle gradations of color. As exemplified by works from this series, the warp and weft are Matson's paintbrush.

Matson's work rewards careful looking—there is more beyond the surface, as the language of weaving takes over, or what she likes to call the phenomenon of the "slow burn." Her woven pictures also evoke a guiding textile forebear, Anni Albers, and her concept of pictorial weavings, or handwoven textiles made as artworks to be hung on a wall. This model is demonstrated by a work like *Pasture* (fig. 2), in which woven textures compose the picture plane.[4] By assigning titles to objects of craft, Albers offered these woven wall hangings as artworks worthy of aesthetic contemplation. She proposed the following:

To let threads be articulate again
and find a form for themselves to no other end

Fig. 2 Anni Albers, *Pasture*, 1958. Cotton, 14 × 15½ in. The Metropolitan Museum of Art, Purchase, Edward C. Moore Jr. Gift, 1969

Fig. 3 Jean Stamsta, *13 Acres*, 1966. Wool on rayon, 45½ × 43 × 4½ in. Milwaukee Art Museum, Museum Purchase

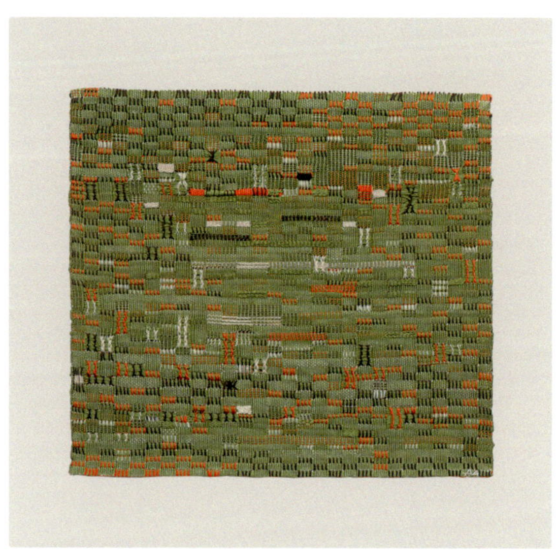

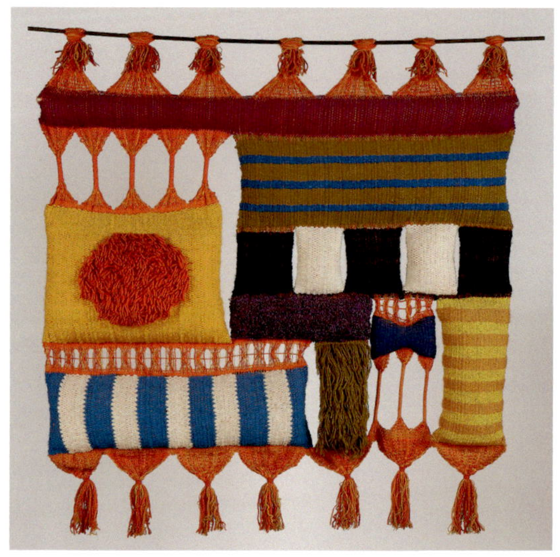

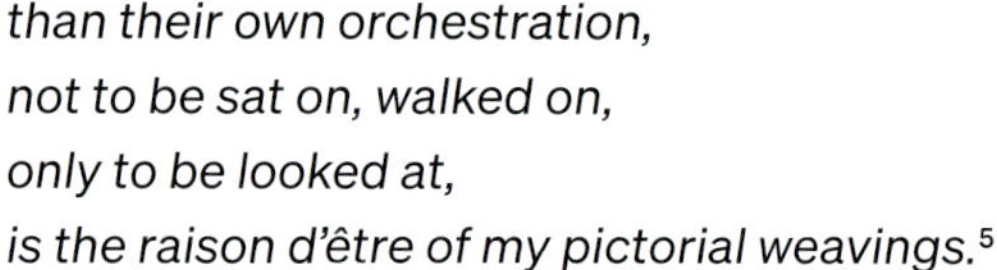

than their own orchestration,
not to be sat on, walked on,
only to be looked at,
is the raison d'être of my pictorial weavings.[5]

Following this statement, Albers also wrote about the importance of tactility in the surface quality of the material.[6] Similarly for Matson, the appearance, or visualization, of her work is directly linked to the tactile qualities of various materials. Matson's complex craft is best explored technically and critically, as her textiles are often about the structures and forms of textiles, creating a meta-discourse. Additionally, the subject matter is often simultaneously historical and contemporary. Matson is a meticulous researcher, studying historic weave structures, patterns, and ways of making, which is made manifest in her woven pictures that are decidedly current.

Since 1982 the Milwaukee Art Museum has invited "artists who have recently come to public attention and who are challenging or expanding the definition of art in our time" to participate in the *Currents* series.[7] Christy Matson is the first weaver represented in *Currents*, which also speaks to the present state of textiles within contemporary art. Wisconsin has a rich tradition of textiles and weaving, with the University of Wisconsin–Madison's home economics department (today the School of Human Ecology) offering courses in textiles beginning in the 1910s. Craft institutions, such as the Wisconsin Society of Applied Arts (later the Wisconsin Designer Craftsmen and today the Wisconsin Designer Crafts Council), founded in 1916, ensured that local craftspeople were supported through meetings and exhibition opportunities, including annual exhibitions at the Milwaukee Art Institute (later the Milwaukee Art Center and now the

Milwaukee Art Museum). In fact, the Museum purchased works from some of these annual exhibitions, including Jean Stamsta's prize-winning *13 Acres* wall hanging from the *46th Annual Wisconsin Designer Craftsmen* show (fig. 3). The Milwaukee Art Museum's 1986 exhibition *Fiber R/Evolution* examined the field of fiber using the language of fine art, arguing that meaningful distinctions between craft and art were inconsequential.[8] Many of the Museum's fiber works were acquired following this show, including Ed Rossbach's *Tubular Construction* (fig. 4) and *Raffia Basket and Pitcher* (1973), Lia Cook's *Hanging Net* (1984), Gerhardt Knodel's *Souvenir* (1982), Walter Nottingham's *Celibacy* (1966–67), Lenore Tawney's *Wild Grass* (1957), Dorian Zachai's *Dog* (1959), and Claire Zeisler's *High Rise* (1983–84). It is against this backdrop that the Milwaukee Art Museum has invited Christy Matson to explore the current boundaries of the textile medium, as her practice participates in the development of contemporary art and craft.

After completing a BFA in studio art with a concentration in fiber, learning hand-weaving as an undergraduate at the University of Washington, Matson met influential textile pioneer Lia Cook at The Jacquard Center in North Carolina. Soon thereafter, she began studying with Cook, which forever changed her artistic practice as she discovered the basics of digital weaving on a Jacquard loom. As part of her graduate work, she began depicting the sound of weaving visually by making spectrograms, using the looms as her subject matter, and then translating the images into

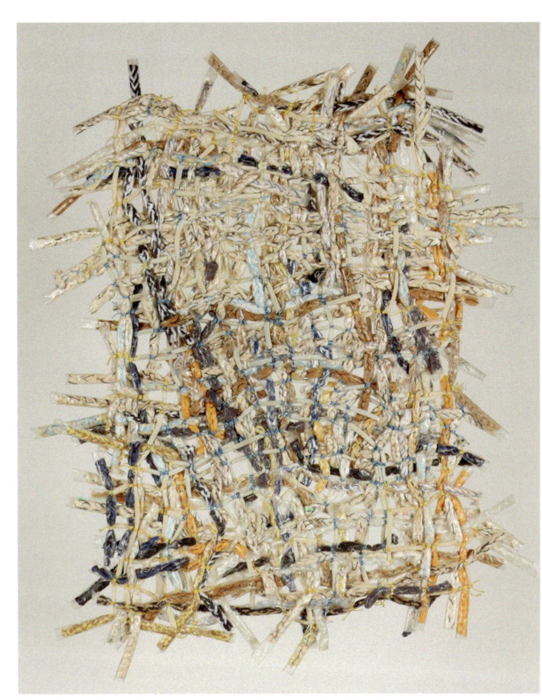

Fig. 4 Ed Rossbach, *Tubular Construction*, 1969. Polyethylene tubing, rayon, and cotton, 40 × 34 in. Milwaukee Art Museum, Gift of Floyd and Dorothy Segel

patterns via coding software.[9] It was this early work combining weaving with sound elements that garnered her national attention, leading to participation in such exhibitions as *40 Under 40: Craft Futures* (2012) at the Renwick Gallery, Smithsonian American Art Museum, which was the first museum to acquire Matson's work.[10] While this early work conceptually explored the sound of textiles, her practice has continued to develop in new directions.

As historian Leora Auslander has noted, textile productions (spinning, weaving, knitting, quilting) have been considered highly feminized forms of labor, and the textiles produced by these methods have been used to construct gender.[11] Making textiles provides unlimited choices: How to construct? Which

Fig. 5 *Coverlet*, 1830–49. Cotton and wool, 75 × 64 in. Helen Louise Allen Textile Collection, School of Human Ecology, University of Wisconsin–Madison

Optics, 2018 (detail)

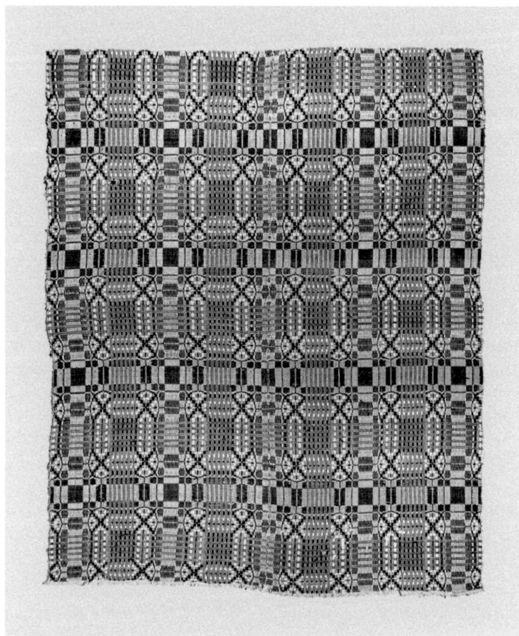

structure to use? And what about materials? But the legacy of textiles as associated with "women's work" is something that is not lost on Matson as an artist who participates in this continuum that has lasted for thousands of years and across global cultures. Matson's work bears the imprint of gendered labor, and her woven pictures provide the contemporary viewer with a way to engage with textiles from the past in thoughtful and innovative ways. Similar to Sheila Hicks and Lenore Tawney, and like fiber artists from the 1960s, who, as craft historian Elissa Auther has noted, "disregarded the low cultural connotations… utility, femininity, domesticity, amateurism, decorativeness, and even primitiveness," Matson has fashioned an interest in the process of making (in her case, on a digital Jacquard loom) while having direct contact with materials, all in service of experimentation and creativity.[12]

Matson works at the intersection of the past, conducting research on historical weave structures and decorative motifs, and the present, contemplating how to disrupt previous techniques in order to make her weavings resonate for today's audience. As an example, her ongoing investigation into overshot weaving provides some insights into her craft. Begun in 2018, these works reference nineteenth-century American coverlets (fig. 5) constructed in the overshot woven structure (plain weave with supplementary pattern weft). It is no wonder that these geometric woven wonders continue to fascinate Matson, as they clearly express creativity on the part of the weaver, who can fashion them in countless color and pattern variations. *Optics* (facing page) and *Optics II* (see page 4) investigate a geometric pattern sometimes named double bow-knot that offers eye-dizzying optical effects.[13] In Matson's interpretation she layers alternate geometries—red crosses that border on irregularity and three slender, variegated banner-like triangles—that unsettle the ground and offer new aesthetic dimensions. These shapes also reference a universal visual language that Matson explores throughout her textiles.

This recent work questions ideas of memory and imagination through historic weave structures and textile techniques. Another example from the overshot series is *Disruption* (page 20), which, true to its title, disrupts the

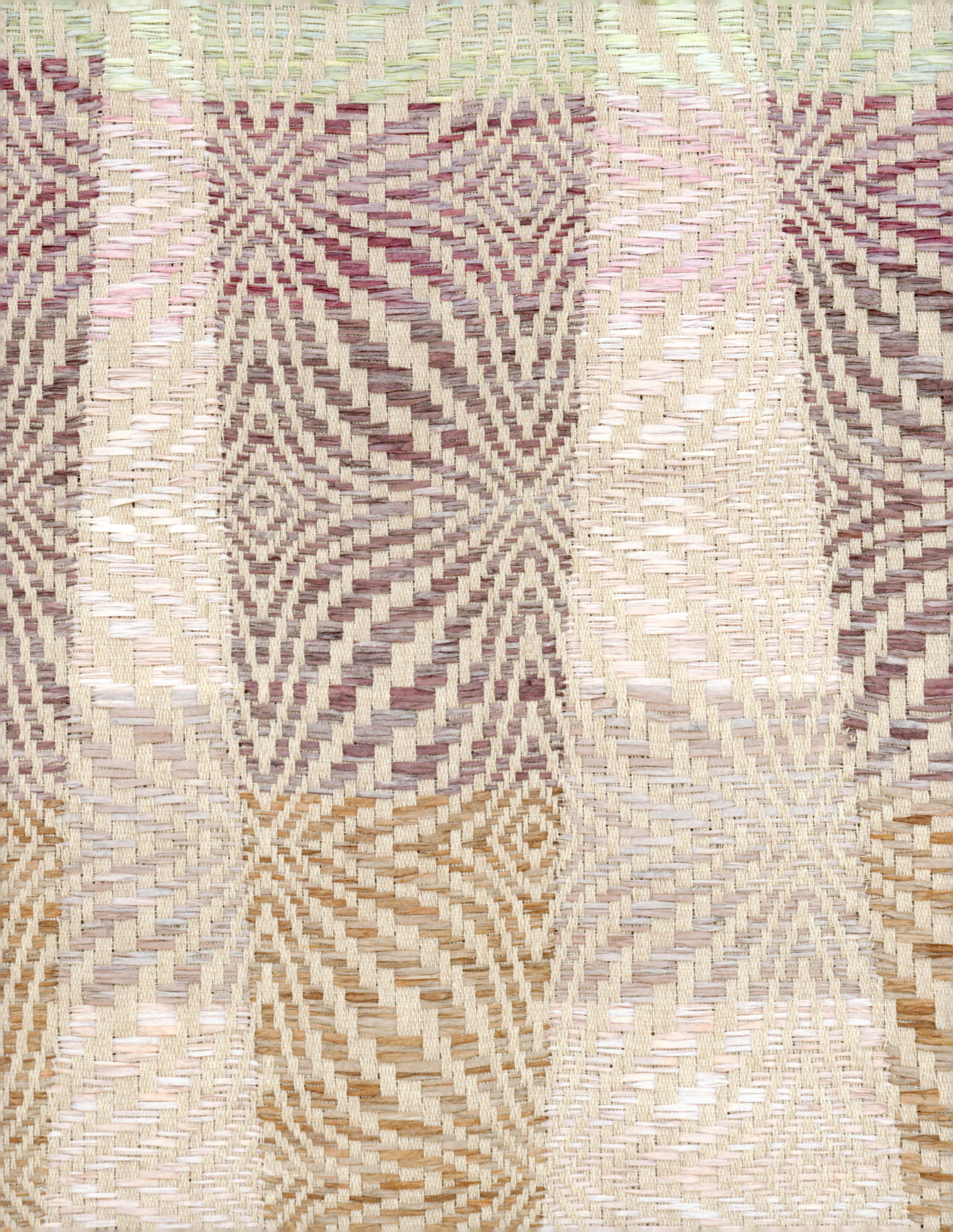

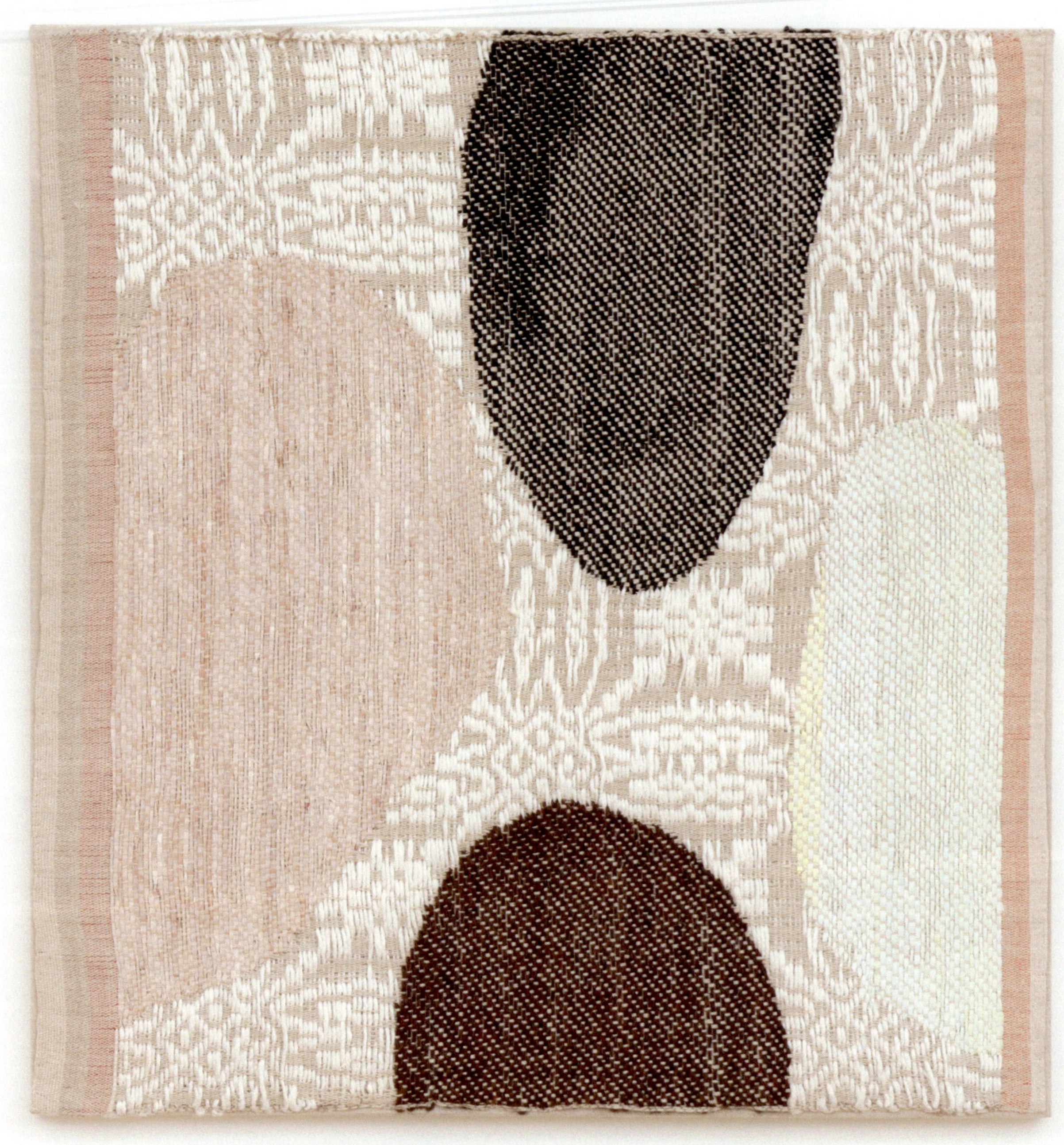

Disruption, 2018

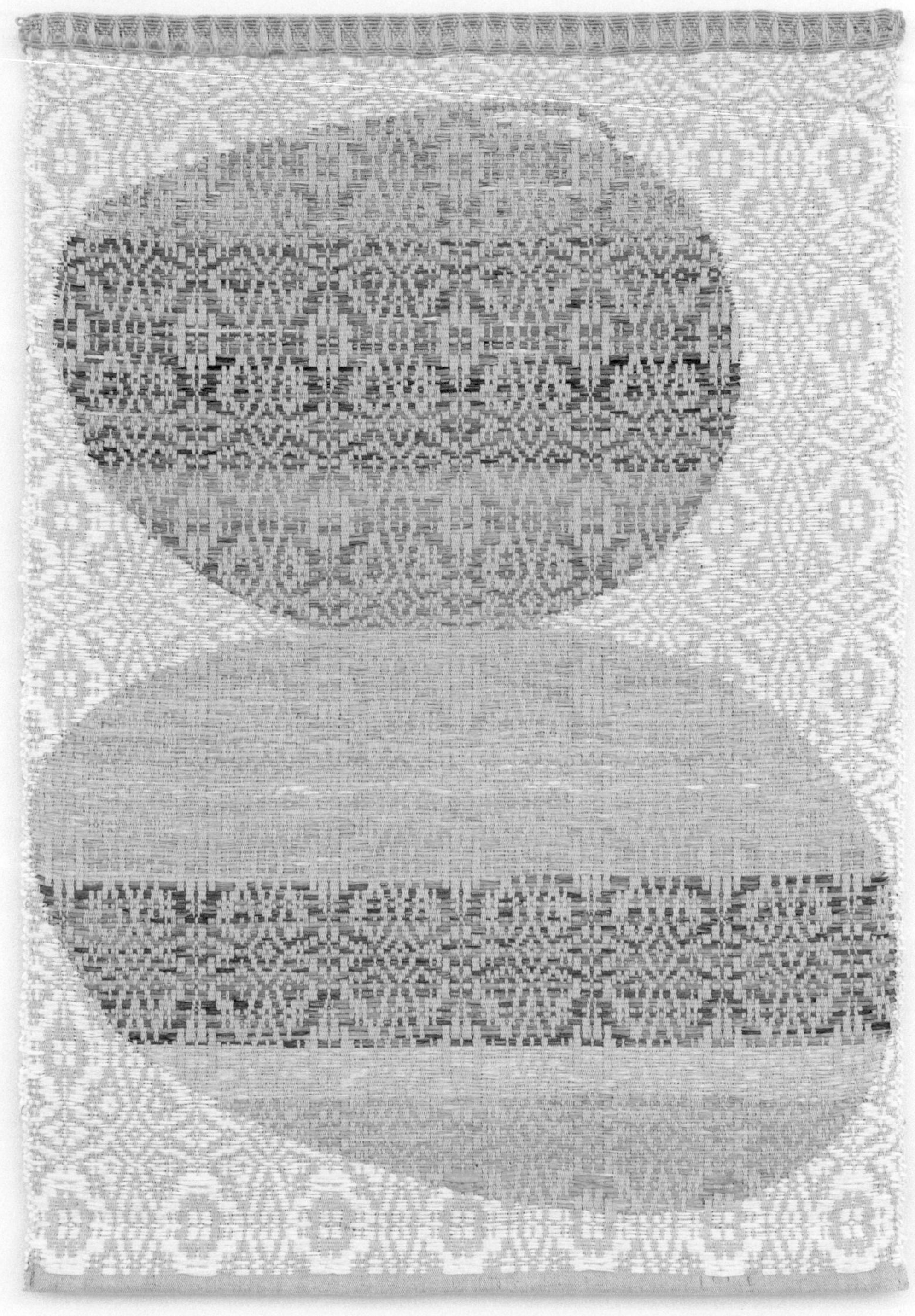

Stack, 2018

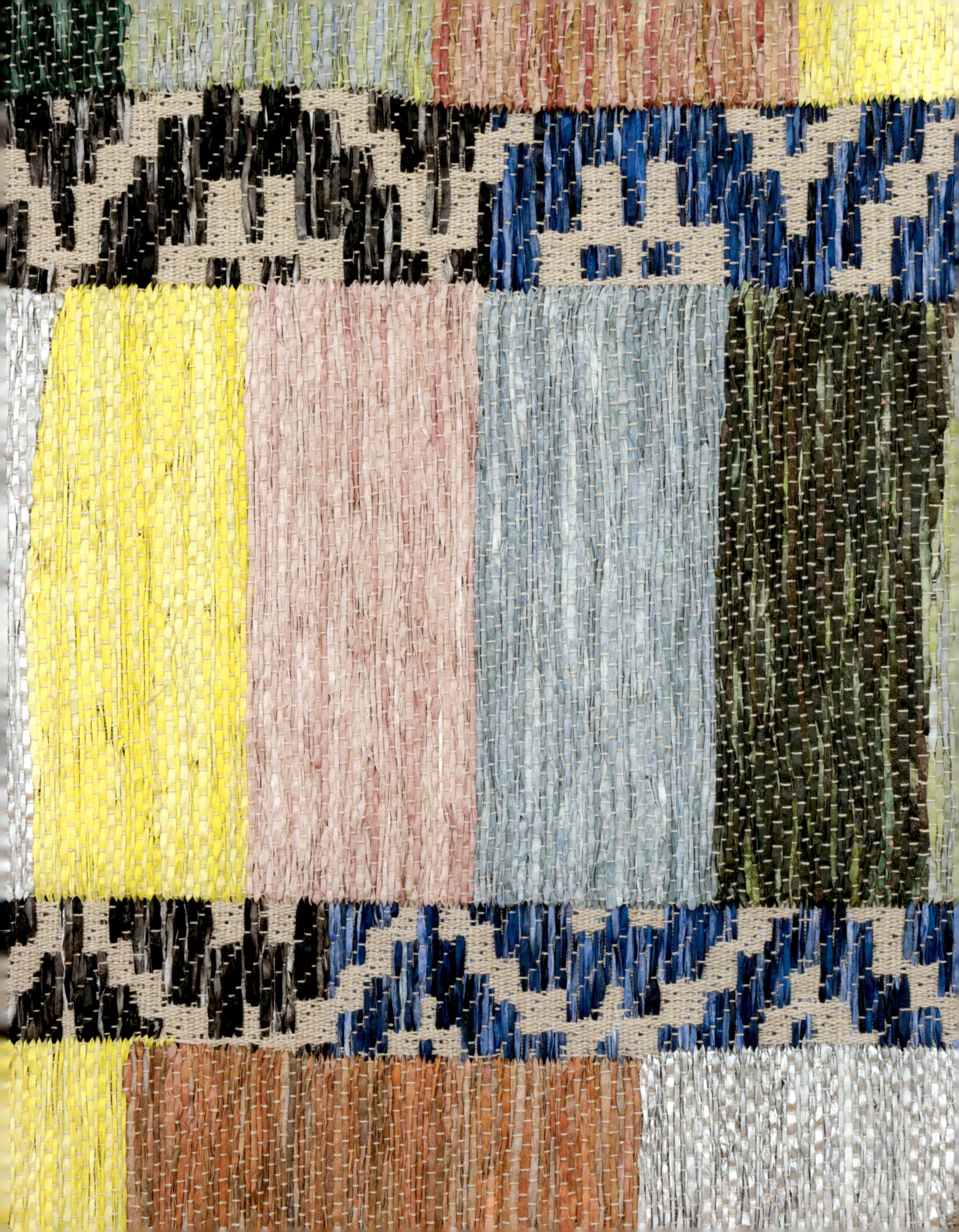

Overshot Variation I, 2018 (detail)

Fig. 6 Dorothy Liebes, drapery fabric sample, 1949. Cotton, wool, rayon, silk, and metal foil laminated in cellulose acetate film, bands of plain and twill weaves, 9⅛ × 8¼ in. Art Institute of Chicago, Gift of Dorothy Liebes Design, Inc.

(Overleaf) Fig. 7 Installation view of Christy Matson, *Untitled I (for Ashgabat)*, 2016–19 (8 of 16 panels). Handwoven cotton, linen, wool, indigo dye, and acrylic on stretched canvas, 90 × 120 × 2 in. Courtesy of Art in Embassies, US Department of State

seemingly traditional ground with four globular shapes jutting in from the sides. These irregularly shaped, cropped lozenges in brown, pink, and yellow obscure the ground, as opposed to Matson's treatment of the two stone-like orbs in *Stack* (page 21), in which the background is uninterrupted yet distorted, as if the shapes are transparent overlays. Within the many works from this series, Matson explores the conventions of the overshot coverlet, expanding and contracting, pushing and pulling to dislocate the highly structured pattern. She then adds her mark—weaving in painterly regions of color—another sign that this is a contemporary work.

In works like *Overshot Variation I* (facing page), Matson's technique collapses two specific textile traditions: the nineteenth-century coverlets woven in the overshot pattern and modern weaving that embraced color and experimental materials, such as those exhibited by California-born New York designer Dorothy Liebes. Liebes was known for incorporating bright colors and unusual, often synthetic, materials in her textile designs (fig. 6). Just as Liebes's synthetic fabrics sparkle, Matson's fields of color coruscate, due to the brilliant metallic and spray-painted papers woven into the textile.

Like Anni Albers's investigations of Indigenous textiles, especially works from Latin America, Matson's weavings also engage threads from this methodology. Another example of Matson mining the history of textiles for appropriate influences for particular works is a commissioned embassy project that

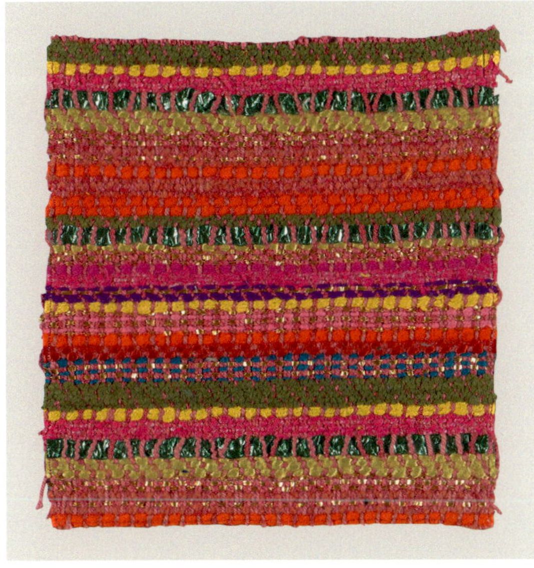

she recently completed. With the goal of fostering cross-cultural diplomacy for the US Embassy in Ashgabat, Turkmenistan, Matson examined sixteenth- to eighteenth-century textiles from Central Asia, including those held by the Art Institute of Chicago, the Cooper Hewitt, Smithsonian Design Museum in New York, the Los Angeles County Museum of Art, and the Helen Louise Allen Textile collection at the University of Wisconsin–Madison. Taking cues from the objects themselves, such as patchwork motifs from women's and children's garments, Matson embarked on a collage of motifs for sixteen monumentally sized textiles for an embassy setting within a foreign country (fig. 7), providing a new language for Silk Road textiles that takes multiple viewpoints into consideration. According to the artist, her experience (as a mother) and the aesthetic (certain shapes, colors, and patterns) that

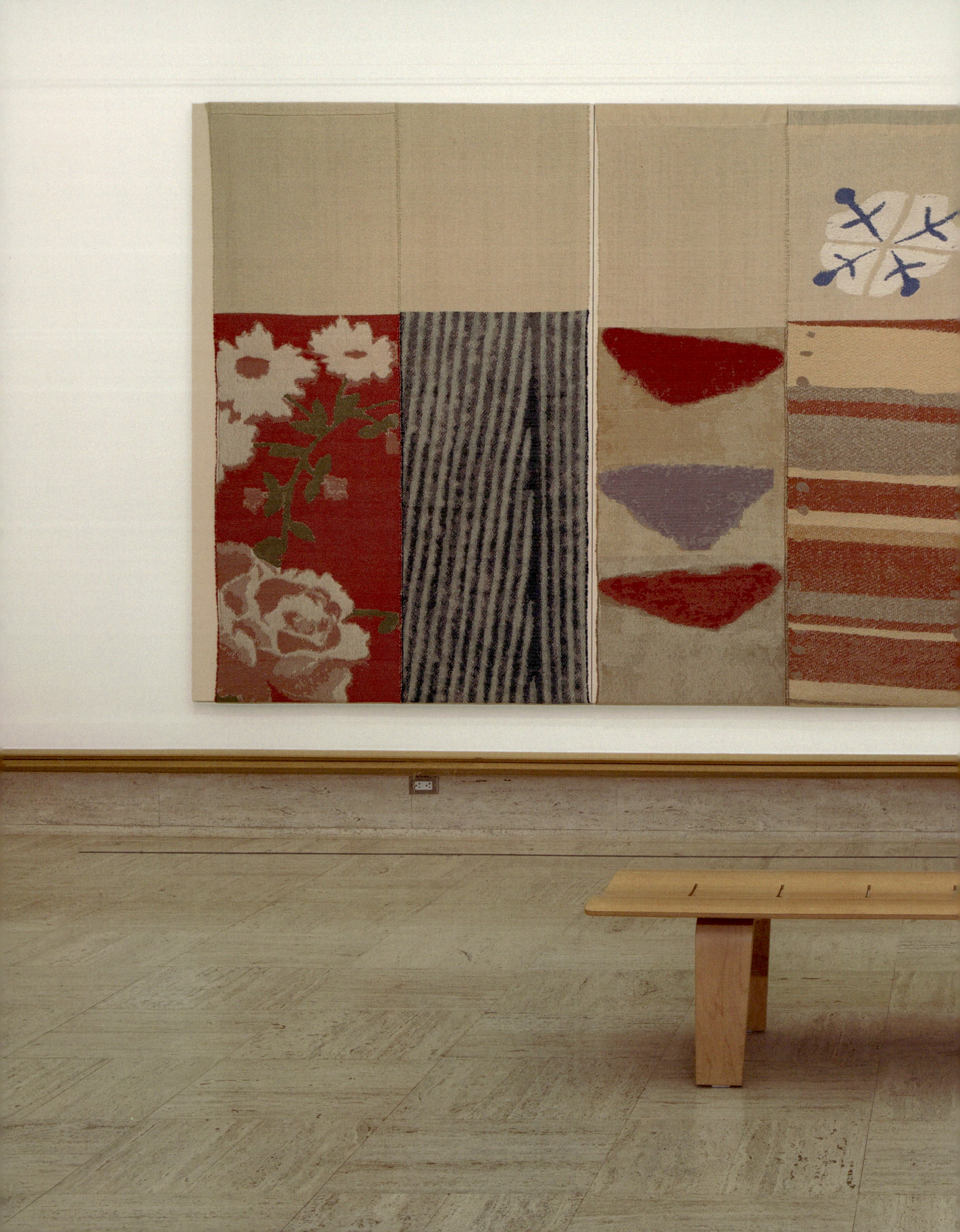

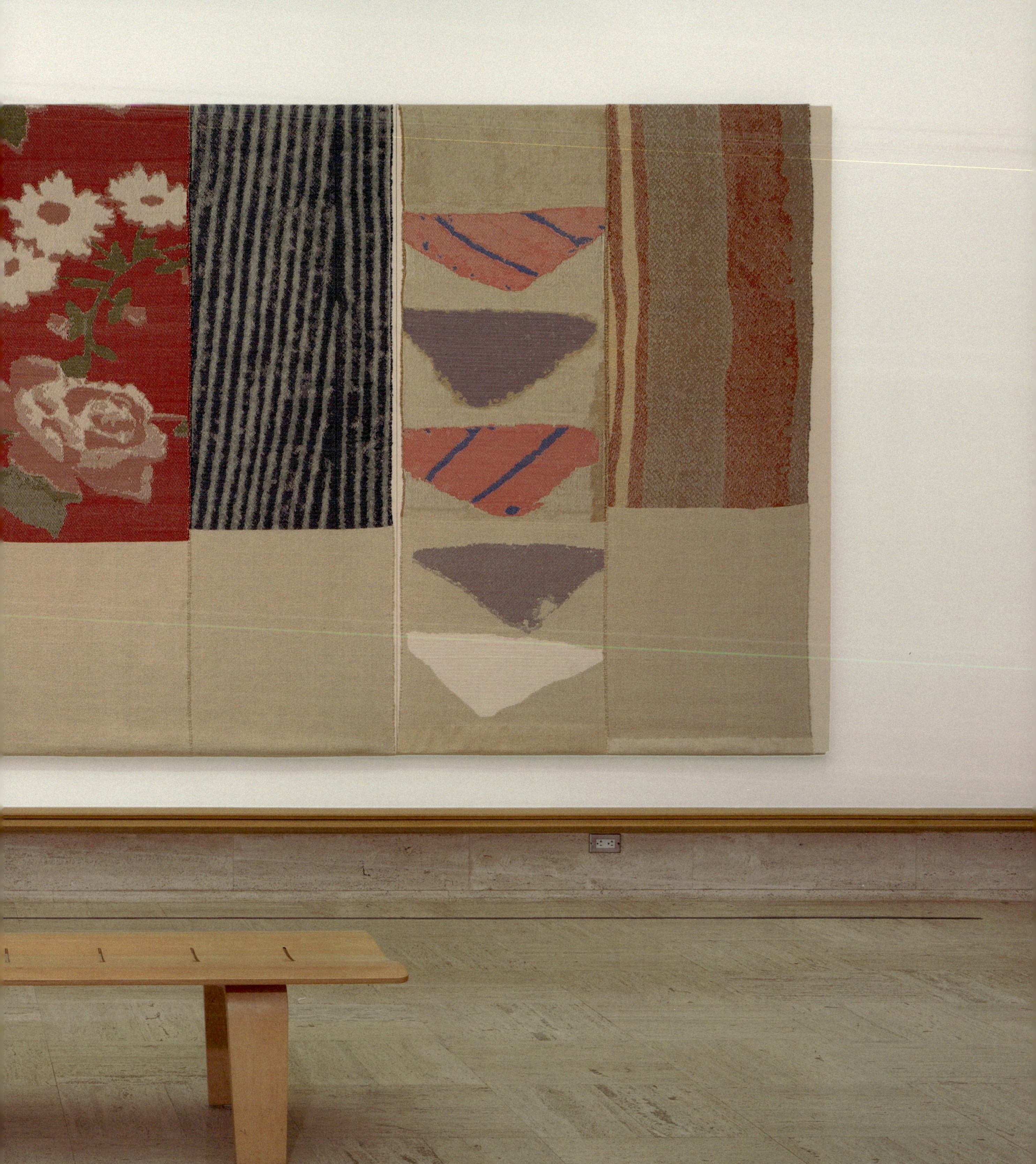

Many Horizons, 2020

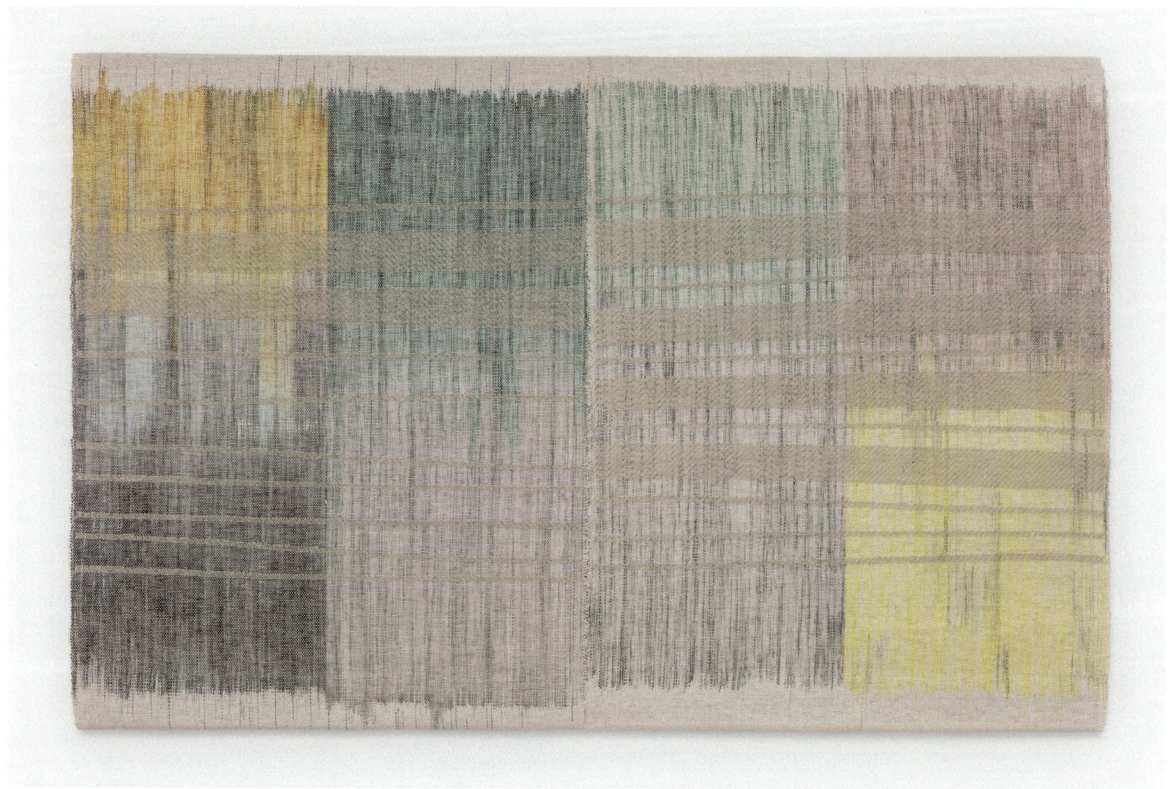

she found through her research were manifested in the work as a collage of ideas and visual elements.

Within the structure of her textiles, she offers a space for experimentation—the fibers spray-painted in metallic and neon colors are one example of this methodology. White Japanese paper yarn given to Matson many years ago by her former professor Lia Cook has been used to varying degrees as a fiber in some of her work. This use of paper also connects her practice with another predecessor, Ed Rossbach, who was a pioneer in the use of nontraditional textile materials, including paper, in his compositions. In fact, Cook studied with Rossbach in the early 1970s at a time when textiles were firmly rooted in the studio craft movement in the Bay Area. Later, when Cook taught Matson in the early 2000s, she professed a model of innovation in handweaving—which also included painting directly on textiles—alongside new technologies like the digital Jacquard loom that had recently emerged. Just as the Jacquard loom's invention in the nineteenth century in France catalyzed paradigmatic changes in textile design and production, its digital descendant is democratizing the field two hundred years later.

Matson follows in a long line of makers who have integrated new technologies into their craft. Cynthia Schira (whom Matson met while in North Carolina) was an early pioneer, using a thirty-two-harness Macomber loom with an embedded computer chip to fashion complicated works that incorporated several weave structures to create abstracted woven patterns.[14] Of course, Lia Cook also wove using technology, and helped shape a viable model for Matson's practice. As artist (and another Cook student) L. J. Roberts has noted, "Cook displaces the stereotype of craft even as she simultaneously reclaims it."[15] Additionally, Cook's textiles create cultural links to the past, as they are "conceived, constructed, and expressed through the history and language of textiles."[16] It is directly from this lineage that Matson's work emerges.

By harnessing the technology of the TC2 digital Jacquard loom, Matson explores the machinery of weaving while also strongly embracing the handwork implicit in working with fibers to create painterly effects in her woven work. Her process involves multiple painstaking steps. Matson first creates an image, then uploads it to a computer. After many hours of drafting structures for each color (every pixel of the pattern is programmed), she relays the coded pattern to the TC2. While weaving, Matson inserts wefts of varying fibers by hand, demonstrating a respect for the labor of the hand that has been implicit in weaving for centuries. Decisions about thread placement are made at every turn, making weaving an exacting artistic process. This digital tool renders Jacquard weaving more accessible, allowing for material and structural exploration while also focusing on skillful making. Textile artist Grethe Sørensen has remarked that designers and artists with hands in production develop new expressions, as "manual work with thread and construction is essential in order to be able to play with the tactile values embedded in textile."[17] As such, Matson's work presents a way forward: an understanding of the balanced relationship between handmade production and aid through digital technologies—one is not privileged over the other. Jacquard weaving provides a way for digital and material tactile languages to interact with one another seamlessly. The digital loom is both as technically ambitious as industrial production and as liberating as handweaving, thereby providing endless possibilities.

From the mid-nineteenth century onward, craft has been situated as the "other" to the Industrial Revolution's production, which has led to the establishment of a craft-versus-technology dichotomy. Matson's work subverts this relationship. This does not mean that she is abandoning craft skills, which are foundational for the design and production of textiles, but rather that she is harnessing available technology to push her work, and to complicate and interrogate the relationship between the digital and the hand. Theorist David Pye has argued that craft does not mean "made by hand"; tools—such as the TC2 digital Jacquard loom—are required by craftspeople to carry out production.[18] As sociologist Richard Sennett has stated, "the enlightened way to use a machine is to judge its powers, fashion its uses, in light of our own limits rather than the machine's potential," suggesting a symbiotic working relationship.[19] As opposed to thinking about digital process and craft as binary opposites, these contemporary practices are concurrently manifested in the work of Matson. In an era of ever-increasing fear about automation, makers still understand that technology will not replace craft.[20] For art historian Julia Bryan-Wilson, "craft" can be a useful term because it allows for exploration of the "overlaps," and as an unfixed and slippery phrase, it enables us to "make connections between... different subjects."[21] In this way, craft should be considered alongside digital technology—which is an aid, but more than just a tool, because it can fundamentally change the way an artist works.

Additionally, Matson's weavings exist in a postindustrial world in which she engages textiles in a socially responsible way by considering issues surrounding sustainability. The deleterious impact of textile production on the planet is now well known: a vast amount of water is used, materials made of fossil fuels don't disintegrate, and most textiles aren't recycled, thus ending up in landfills. By using discarded yarns, dead stock, and surplus materials as part of her artistic practice, Matson is interested in an economy of materials, as living in California for the past ten years has caused her to consider environmental impact as one of the most pressing issues of our time. I couldn't agree more.

This exhibition surveys the recent work of one artist, Christy Matson, and her weaving, a field that has been long associated with women. Textile historian Mary Schoeser has written that textiles convey vast amounts of information, including technology, agriculture, trade, ritual, language, tribute, art, and personal identity.[22] Matson's work interrogates weaving's gendered history, but it does not end there. Her work oscillates on a continuum between minimalism and intense pattern, neutral tones and extreme brightness, history and the present, hand work and digital technology, certainty and experimentation, painterly surface and material tactility. This imbalance and variety is what makes her woven pictures engaging and current. Fundamentally, Matson has transformed the traditional medium of textiles into a contemporary manifestation through experimentation with methods of digital production and new modes of expression. Her work is simultaneously the past and the future.

Notes

1. Anni Albers, *On Weaving*, rev. ed., with afterword by Nicholas Fox Weber and contributions by Manuel Cirauqui and T'ai Smith (1965; repr., Princeton, NJ: Princeton University Press in association with the Josef and Anni Albers Foundation, 2017), 54.

2. Recent exhibitions have explored the disintegrating hierarchy between fine art and craft, including *Anni Albers*, co-organized by the K20, Kunstsammlung Nordrhein-Westfalen, Düsseldorf, and the Tate Modern, London (2018), and *Making Knowing: Craft in Art, 1950–2019* at the Whitney Museum of American Art, New York (2019).

3. "Language as Still Life," conversation between Valerie Amend and Beryl Korot, *Nichons-nous dans l'Internet*, no. 10 (2019): 14. The author would like to thank Christy Matson for this reference.

4. Matson's work was part of *Material Meaning: A Living Legacy of Anni Albers* (2019) at Craft in America Center, Los Angeles, which explored the influence of Albers on contemporary textiles in America.

5. Anni Albers, *Pictorial Weavings* (Cambridge, MA: Massachusetts Institute of Technology, 1959), n.p.

6. Albers, *On Weaving*, 45.

7. Gerald Nordland, *Richard DeVore, 1972–1982* (Milwaukee: Milwaukee Art Museum, 1983), n.p.

8. Milwaukee Art Museum, *Fiber R/Evolution* (Milwaukee: Milwaukee Art Museum in association with the University Art Museum, University of Wisconsin–Milwaukee, 1986).

9. One of Matson's sound installations was included in the 2010 exhibition *The New Materiality: Digital Dialogues at the Boundaries of Contemporary Art*, organized by curator Fo Wilson for the Fuller Craft Museum, Brockton, Massachusetts. It traveled to the Milwaukee Art Museum in 2011.

10. Nicholas R. Bell, *40 Under 40: Craft Futures* (Washington, DC: Renwick Gallery, Smithsonian American Art Museum, 2012).

11. Leora Auslander, "Deploying Material Culture to Write the History of Gender and Sexuality: The Example of Clothing and Textiles," *Clio* 40 (2014), https://journals.openedition.org/cliowgh/716.

12. Elissa Auther, "Classification and Its Consequences: The Case of Fibre Art, 2002," in *Craft: Documents of Contemporary Art*, ed. Tanya Harrod (Cambridge, MA: MIT Press in association with Whitechapel Gallery, London, 2018), 163.

13. This pattern has several names, varying by region: for example, "Hickory Leaf" in North Carolina and "Double Muscadine Hulls" in Georgia. Margaret E. White, *Hand-Woven Coverlets in the Newark Museum* (Newark, NJ: Newark Museum, 1947), 19.

14. Janet Koplos and Bruce Metcalf, *Makers: A History of American Studio Craft* (Chapel Hill: University of North Carolina Press, 2010), 469.

15. L. J. Roberts, "Put Your Thing Down, Flip It, and Reverse It," in *Extra/Ordinary: Craft and Contemporary Art*, ed. Maria Elena Buszek (Durham, NC: Duke University Press, 2011), 249.

16. Inez Brooks-Myers, *Lia Cook: Material Allusions* (Oakland: Oakland Museum of California, 1995), 8.

17. Grethe Sørensen, "From Traditional to Digital Tools," *Textile Society of America Symposium Proceedings* (Lincoln: Textile Society of America, University of Nebraska, 2010).

18. David Pye, *The Nature and Art of Workmanship* (Cambridge: Cambridge University Press, 1968), 25.

19. Richard Sennett, *The Craftsman* (New Haven, CT: Yale University Press, 2008), 105.

20. This anxiety has actually been around since the Industrial Revolution, during which the Jacquard loom was invented. The etymology of the term "sabotage" can be traced to this time, when silk weavers in France expressed their fierce opposition to the automation afforded by the loom by throwing a wooden *sabot* (shoe) into the Jacquard mechanism to jam it up because they feared losing their livelihoods.

21. Julia Bryan-Wilson, Liz Collins, Sabrina Gschwandtner, Cat Mazza, and Allison Smith, "The Politics of Craft: A Roundtable," in *The Craft Reader*, ed. Glenn Adamson (London: Bloomsbury, 2010), 628.

22. Mary Schoeser, *Textiles: The Art of Mankind* (New York: Thames and Hudson, 2012).

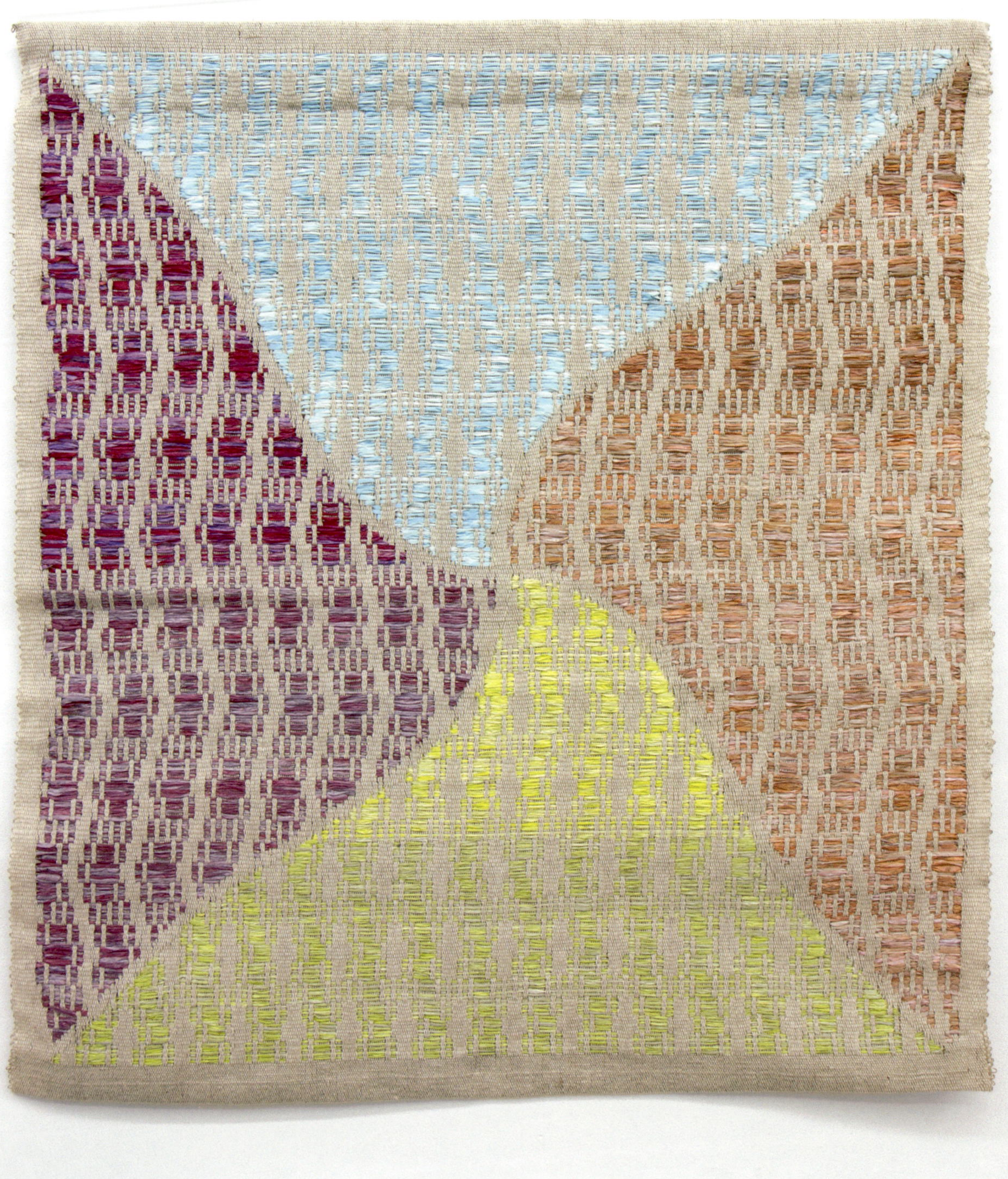

Untitled (Turbine), 2018

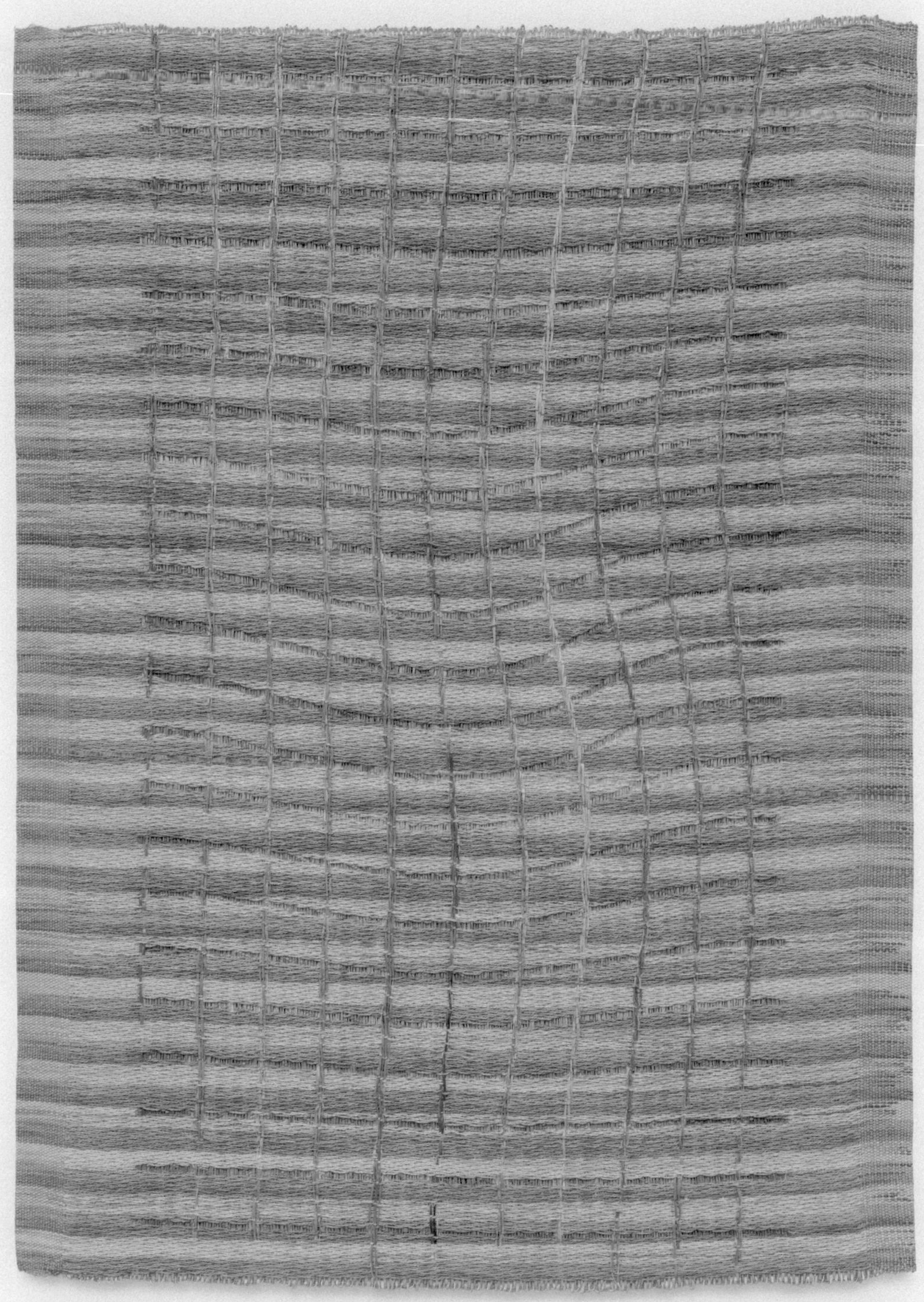

Change of Course (Twisted Grid), 2020

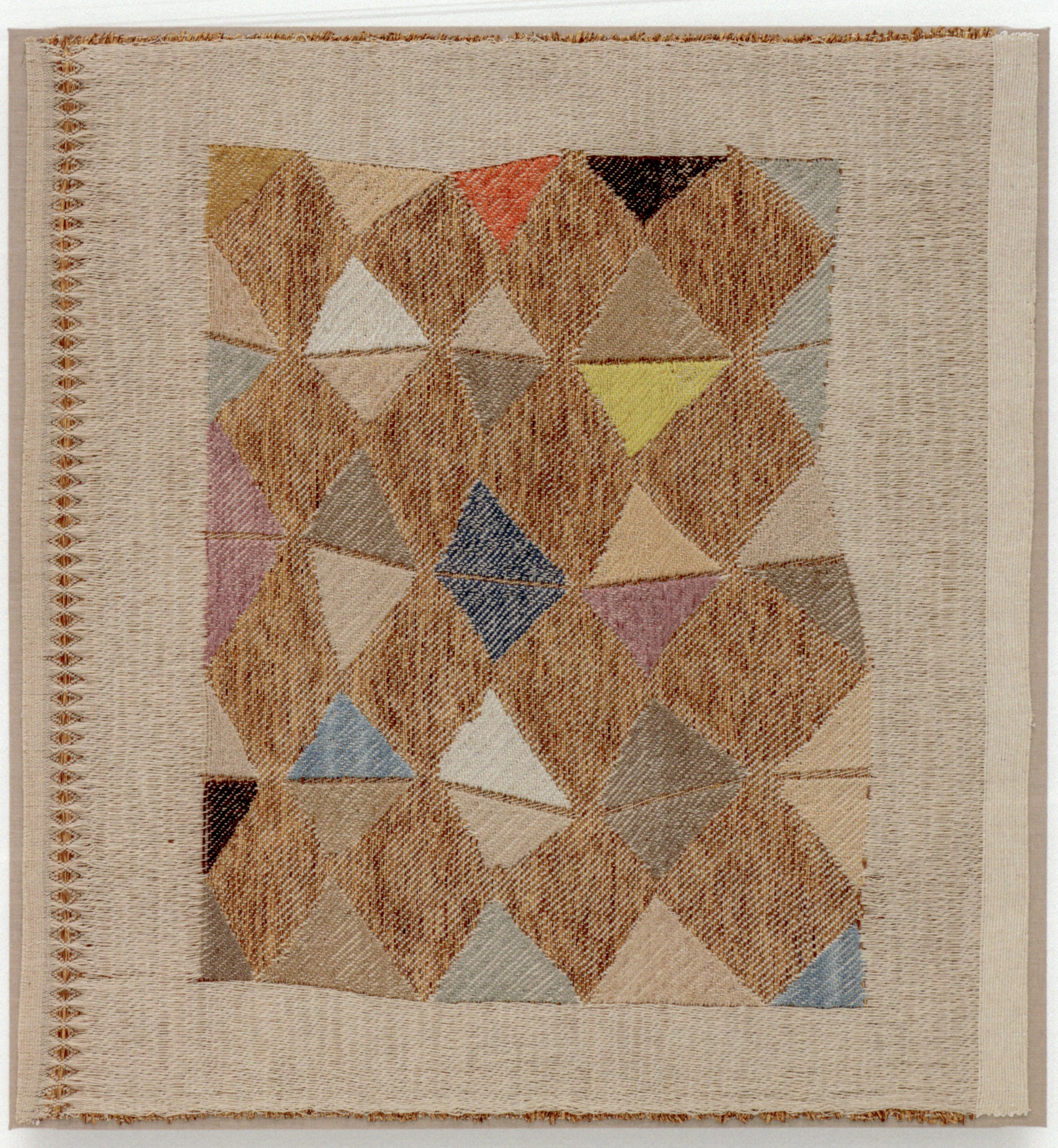

Paragon, 2017

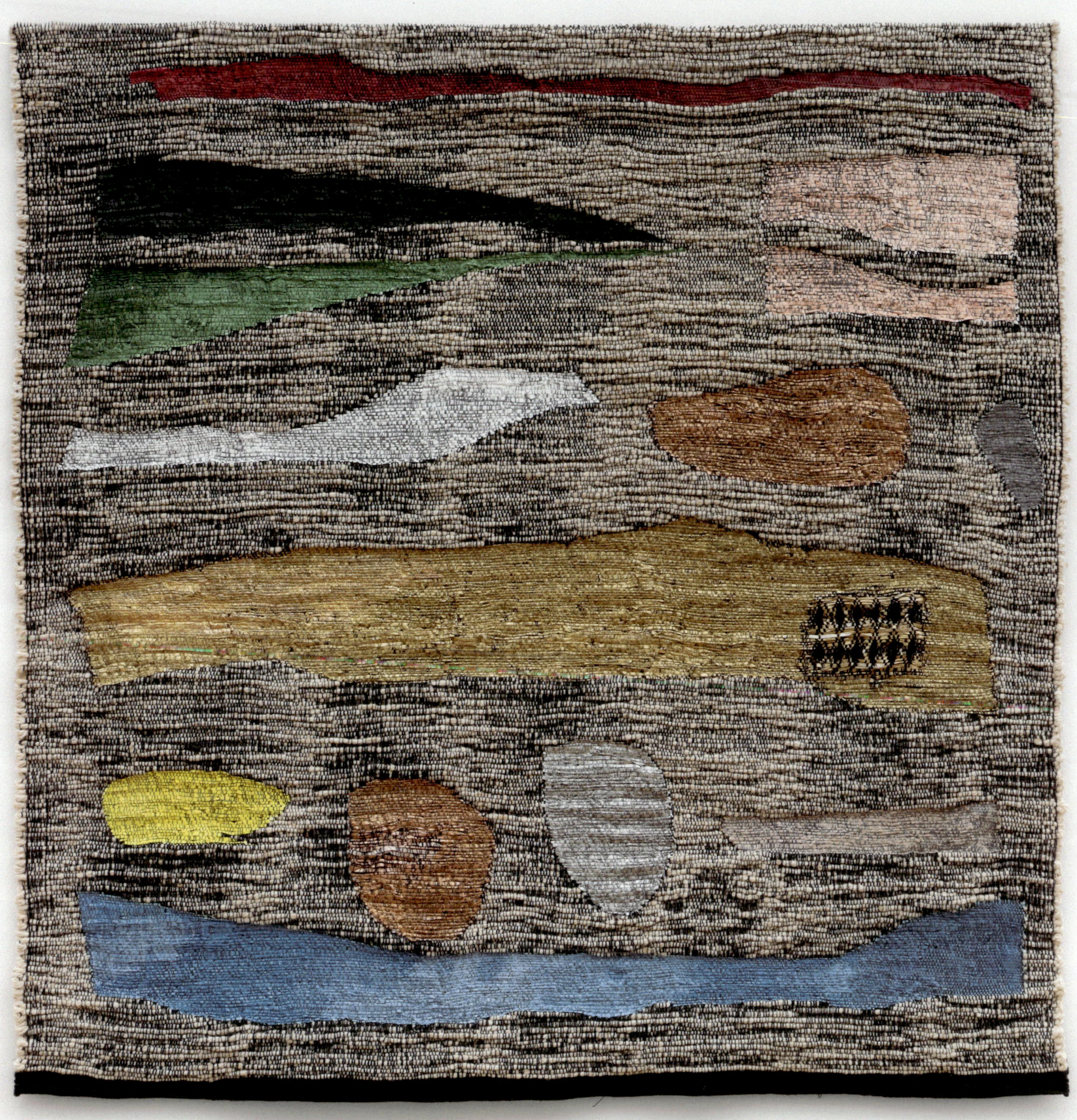

A Complete Thought, 2018

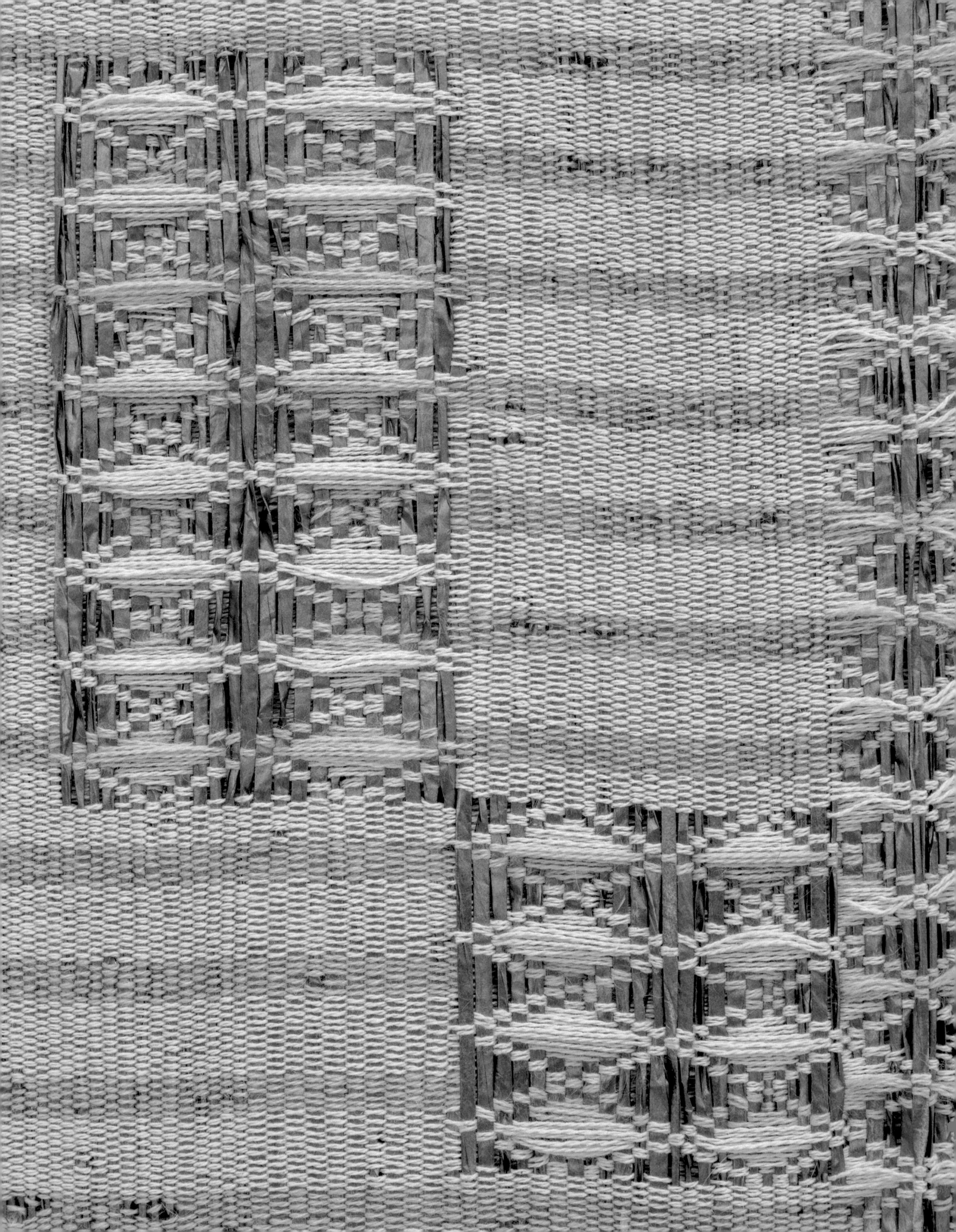

Feel by Sight

Su Wu

One late summer morning in her downtown Los Angeles studio, as we move in and out of the sunlight filtered through factory windows, warming and unwarming ourselves, the artist Christy Matson tells me an apocryphal story about mummy wrappings. Cloth is one of the earliest human inventions, known from the beginning of recorded history across civilizations, but when the tombs were dug up and the bogs turned over, the material was degraded by the elements and "not valuable anyway" to plundering nineteenth-century archaeologists, meaning: not pottery, not gold. Of course, most of what is found on archaeological digs is discarded, surviving pestilence and war only to fall victim to irrelevance. What we know of the fabric of early human life—from the present-day Middle East to Northern Europe—is not from observing large swaths of textile but rather from its impressions, such as what textures the missing pieces left behind in clay, or what fibers sunk into dead bodies over centuries, Matson explains. We declare our values in what we do not keep of the past, and then again in how we attend to gaps in history. In Matson's work, when "function is pulled back into abstraction," as she says of our incomplete memories, the conventions surrounding cloth become radical, part of a consideration of the ever-evolving relationship among avant-garde art, craft, and technology. Her weavings—which are found in the Smithsonian American Art Museum, the Art Institute of Chicago, and the Los Angeles County Museum of Art, among other collections—interrogate the medium of textile itself, gleefully and irreverently dipping into its associations. Nothing is redeemed that was not

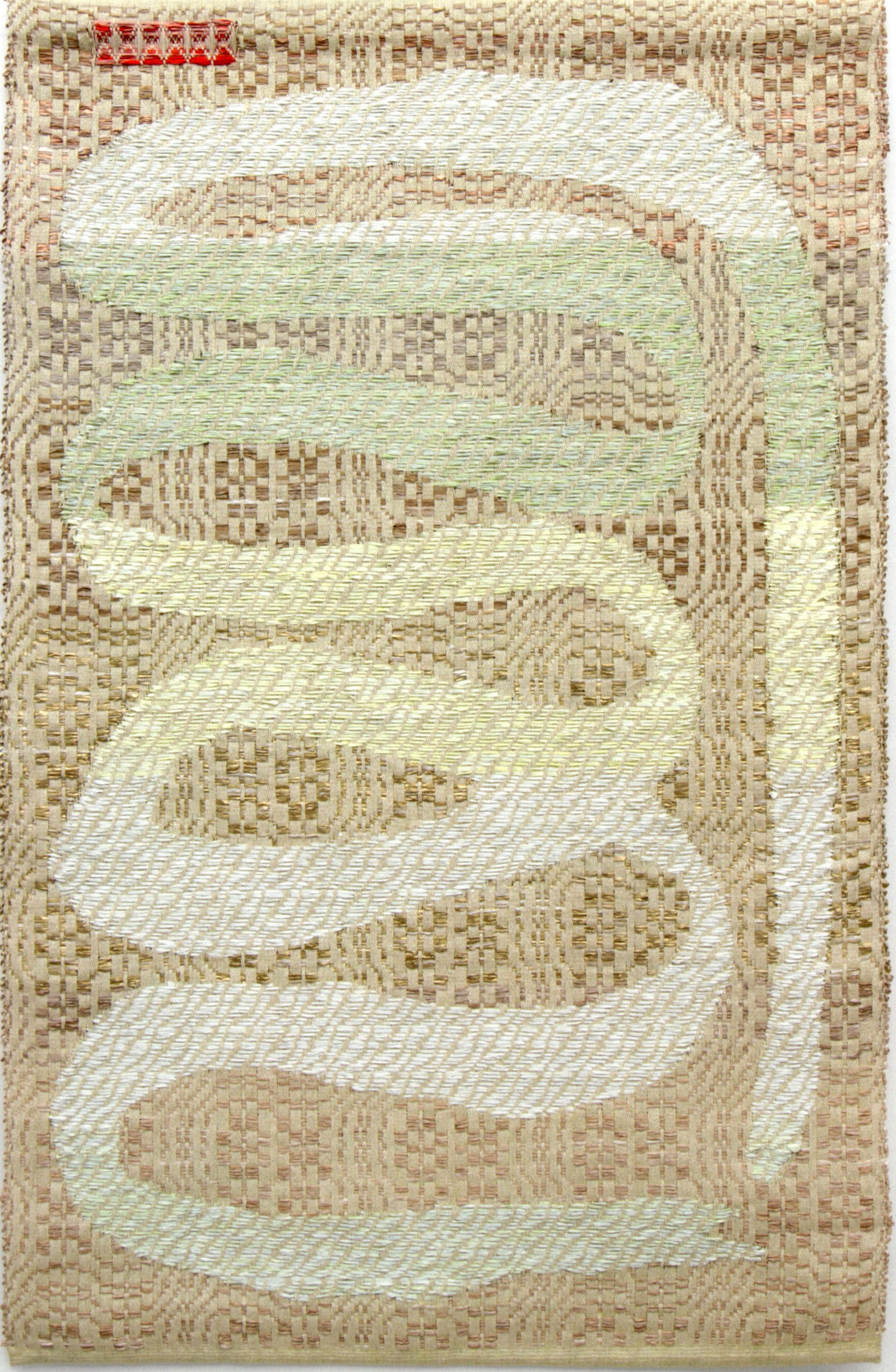

Fig. 8 Dorothea Rockburne, *Silence I*, 1972. Collage, 6 × 4 in. Courtesy of Craig F. Starr Gallery, New York

seeking redemption, not least of all fiber by its adjacency to painting, nor by its adoption by men. This is an artist exploding a form from within. She does it with a sincerity that attends erudition, and with the pleasure of choosing when to downplay proficiency and when to show it off.

In the work *Ouroboros* (facing page), a flourish appears to recede into the material, and the image plane thickens. Matson's pieces, in which she creates both "the image and the substrate for it," thrills with intricacy and depth, and most thrillingly of all with the possibility of the decorative, "a dirty word," Matson laughs. Matson is interested in what weaving can do. *Ouroboros* depicts a snake with a tortuous form, its body winding like the weft that made it. In the top left corner, fingernail-sized red triangles burrow to points, re-creating in slightly enlarged scale an industrial weave once used for diapers, because the thickness created absorbency and warmth. As in the work of Anni Albers, whose graduate thesis at the Bauhaus was a noise-dampening material for an auditorium, Matson investigates where decoration might accompany our invention of tools for living. The lines of the waffled section of *Ouroboros* are a pattern with purpose, and Matson's use of this particular weave conveys feel by sight, or the haptic sense that distinguishes artwork in fiber. The sensation of plushness, of softness and depth, is something a weaving does.

Removed from its intended use, though, the weave pattern is also a latticed grid, one that recalls the geometric explorations of a Sol LeWitt wall drawing or the mathematical inflections of Dorothea Rockburne, whose works similarly hold a place of indeterminacy between painting and sculpture (fig. 8). In Rockburne's installations and wallworks—of folded paper, adhesive labels, furnace oil, shrink-wrap, Ultra Lube LMX Red Grease—the structure of the piece is both a conveyance and the matter, both a mass and an interstice, as Rockburne said in a 1972 interview:

I make parts that make units, and in forming a unit I make combinations. I try not to make useless combinations. . . . After arriving at certain combinations that will in themselves make one unit, I join units, so that a work is a combination of many parts, units and then larger units. This of course comes from math, which deals with combinations of parts and units.[1]

Rockburne, like Matson, does not derive her artwork from any specific mathematical operation, but rather experiments within a bounded equation of her own devising, in which the qualities of the material become the algebraic variable, the (*x*) unknown. In these pieces, the grid is not an unyielding container for our softer, subjective perceptual qualities. As ordinary as in the world itself, the container is an active thing, created and modified by our being in it. "Perception is reciprocity," Matson says. "What you give is also what is given back to you."

Matson is not a nostalgist for some imagined past. She works with naturally dyed threads in organic materials—wool, alpaca, cotton—but also with metal and material given to her over the years, like a few rolls of paper string she received from the American fiber artist (and Matson's former professor) Lia Cook and carried from studio to studio for more than a decade before it made its way into a work. "I am frugal and economical in how I approach material," Matson says. In some instances, she has taken these strings to the roof of her studio and spray-painted them, to create shocking fluorescents. Other threads on her shelf are by-products of industrial processes. "What would a contemporary ethnographic textile look like?" Matson asks me. It might

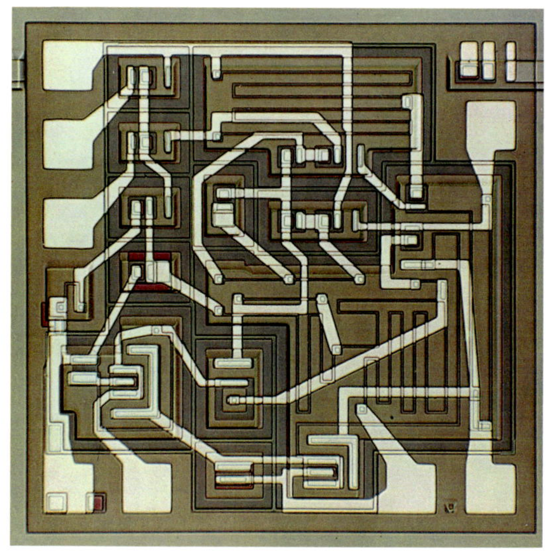

Fig. 9 µA709 operational amplifier, Fairchild Camera and Instrument Corporation, 1965. Courtesy of the Computer History Museum

look like fast fashion, she offers as an answer. She holds out skeins of a linen used to produce high-end denim, the several cones of thread a "treasure" for her, but a negligible amount in manufacturing. "Core memory," she reminds me when I invoke the dreaded factory-made, "is also a weaving." Indeed, the integrated circuits used in early computers, powering calculators and missile-guiding devices, were disproportionately made in factory settings by women, and particularly by women of color, whose nimble fingers and perceived affection for weaving as a traditional craft were racialized as ethnic traits that made native people ideally disposed to manual, nondigital labor. "After years of rug weaving, Indians were able to visualize complicated patterns and could, therefore, memorize complex integrated circuit designs," boasted a spokesperson for Fairchild Semiconductor in 1970, which at the time was both the country's largest semiconductor manufacturer and the largest employer of Indigenous Americans, with nearly one thousand Navajo women working at its plant near Shiprock, New Mexico—before the jobs went overseas (fig. 9).[2] Of course, it is the "women making chips in Asia" whose bodies are imprinted into the "circuit of technoculture" that scholar Donna Haraway famously uses as an example of real-life cyborgs.[3] A weaving, it turns out, can also be suppressed, which depends both on being unseen and constitutive. Despite how much time we stare at screens, we rarely see behind them.

In Matson's *Overshot Variations* series from 2018 on, the separation between weave structure and surface is ever more dizzyingly indistinct (pages 40–43, 64). Sprawling patterns of hashmarks, checkerboards, and grids, almost psychedelic in their effusion, bound across the frame of the image and sometimes off the edge. The patterns are drawn from weave patterns that Matson found in multiple archives across cultures and borders, seemingly without cross-pollination. They reflect a geometric sublime or the "ingenuity of the human brain working its way out over time," as Matson explains, in, say, both present-day Peru and present-day Turkmenistan (where Matson has prepared a multipanel tapestry nearly thirty feet high for the US Embassy in Ashgabat, and which took her four solid months to weave; see fig. 7). Rather than a skimming of culture—a well-founded, well-worn charge leveled at the many modernists who took non-Western imagery in service of their own aesthetic imperialisms—Matson identifies the engineering in the structure of the weave, the very edifice of the too-often-appropriated superficialities. Oversized, the patterns appear from a distance as abstract, graphic compositions but disintegrate upon closer view into another composition, of the threads and their crossings and the small porous gaps in between. A pattern is something a weaving does, and here the pattern writ large is of the overlooked labor, rendered in the very action—the very weave—that the pattern represents abstractly. It is "overshot re-created in overshot"; in other words, "a pattern that emerges from faithful reproduction of technique," as Matson says. The work offers a rousing declaration of image in a digitized moment, as still having the potential to be a materially substantive thing.

And unlike the minimalist sculptors who similarly unyoked material from function, but whose work seemed almost ashamed of the humility of its source and thus roused to the monumental, Matson's art is emphatically about the associations suffused into a material by long human use—she is not trying to break free of the history of fiber nor its humilities. A weaving is also sometimes a diaper, or a shroud for the dead. When Matson embeds the surface of a piece in its framework, she compresses the perceptual distance between what we see and what holds everything up, and brings the substrate to the fore as a motif.

Many years ago, when Matson was the youngest person ever to receive tenure in the Department of Fiber and Material Studies at the School of the Art Institute of Chicago, she

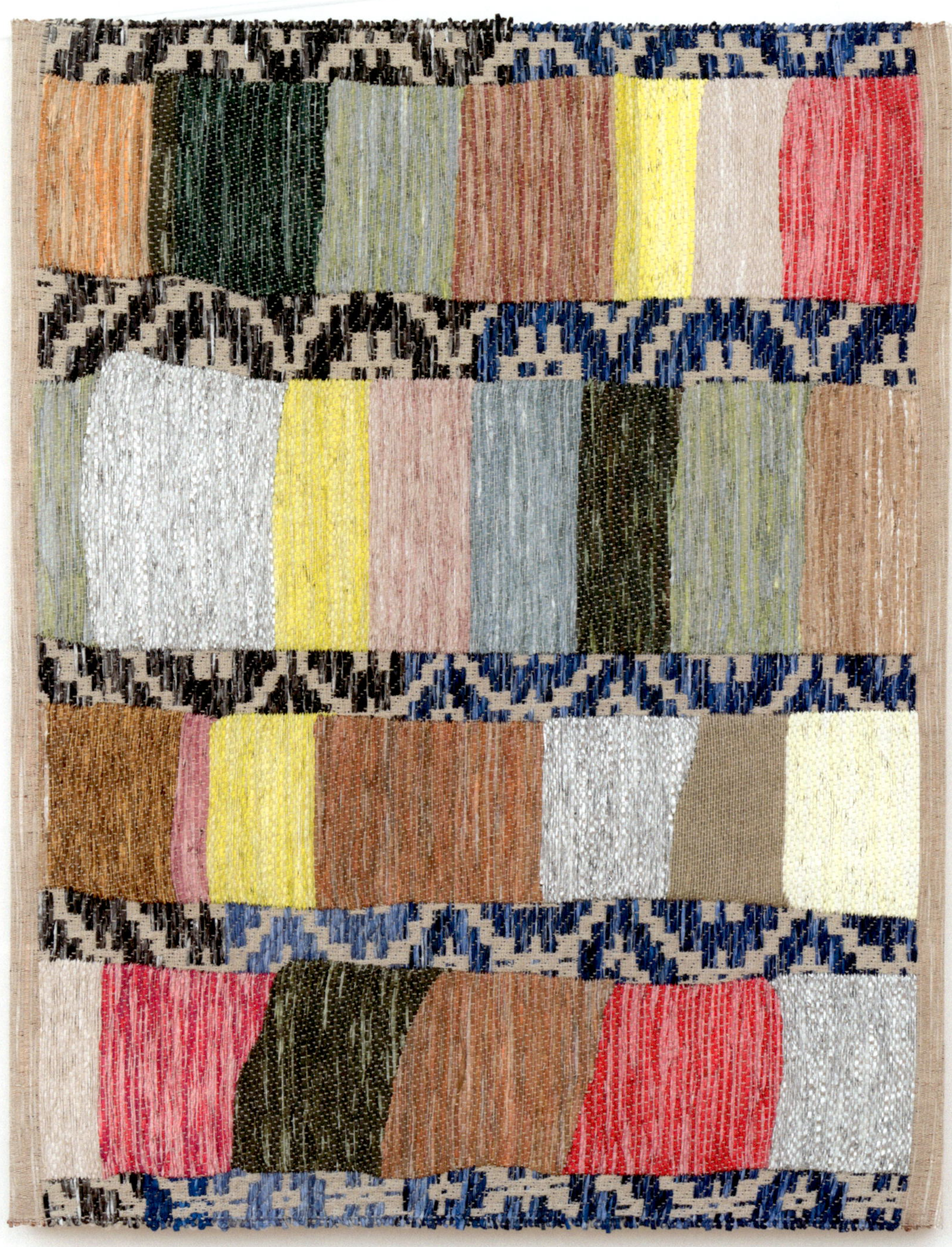

Overshot Variation I, 2018

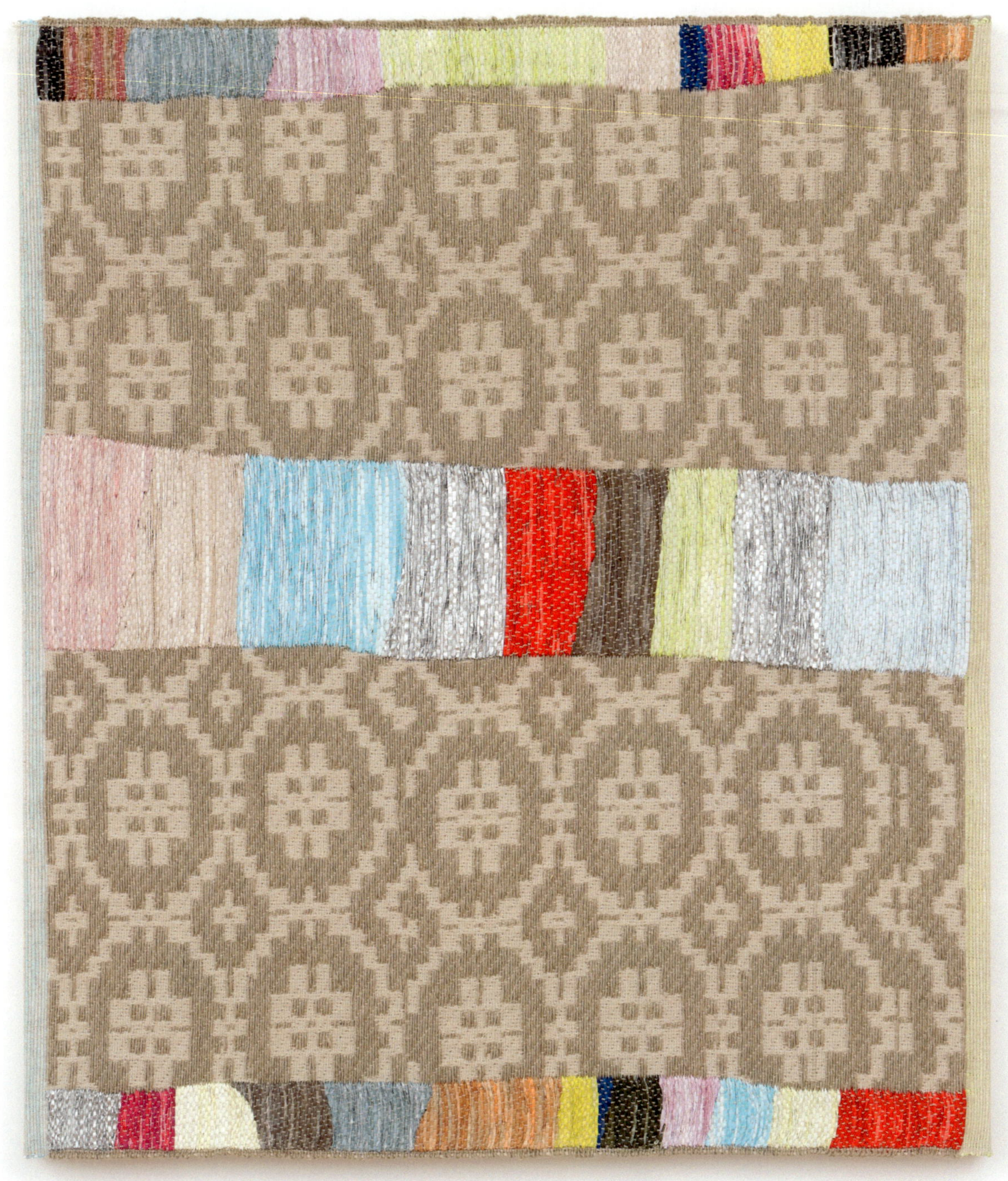

Overshot Variation II, 2018

(Overleaf)
Overshot Variation 3, 2019

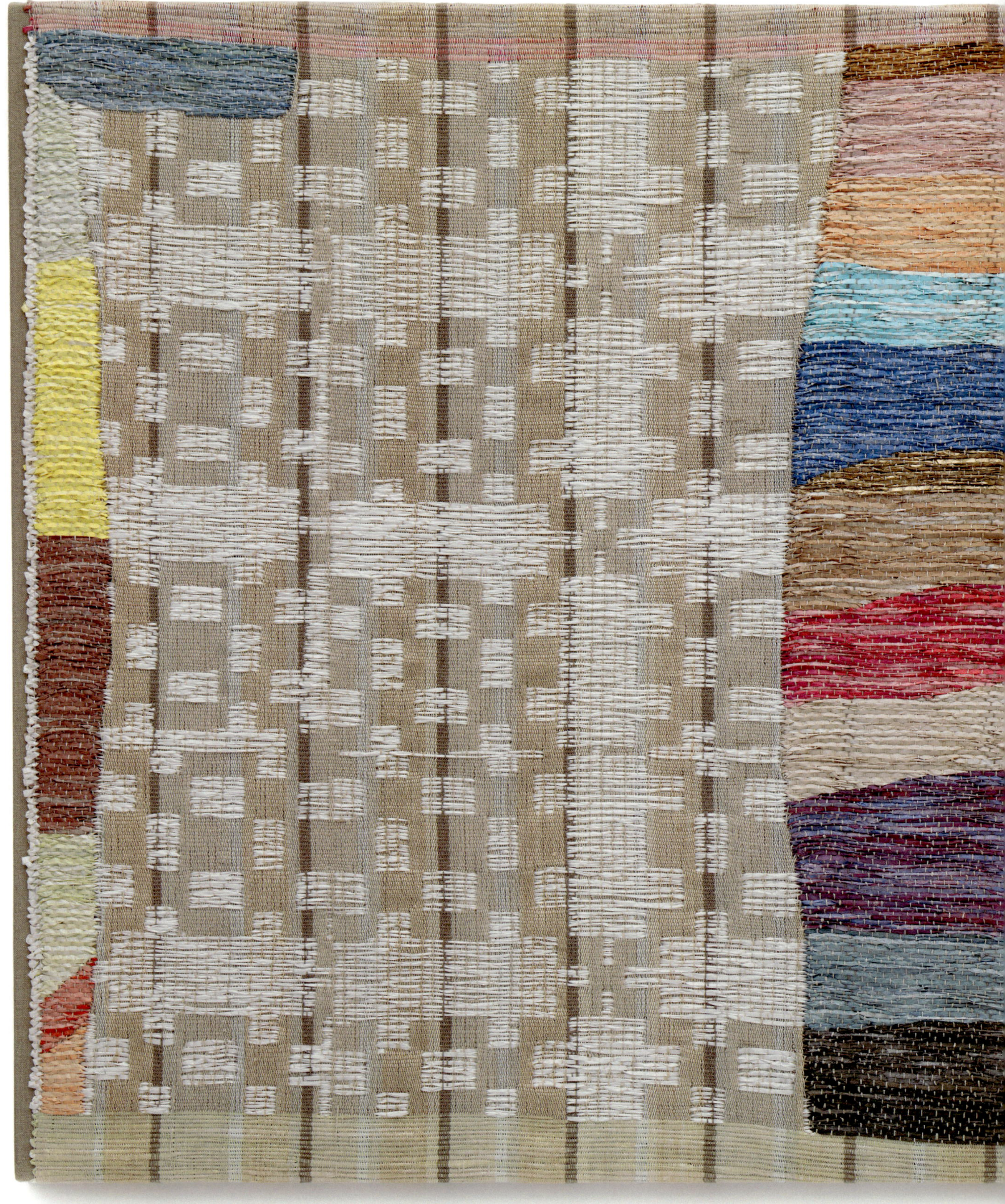

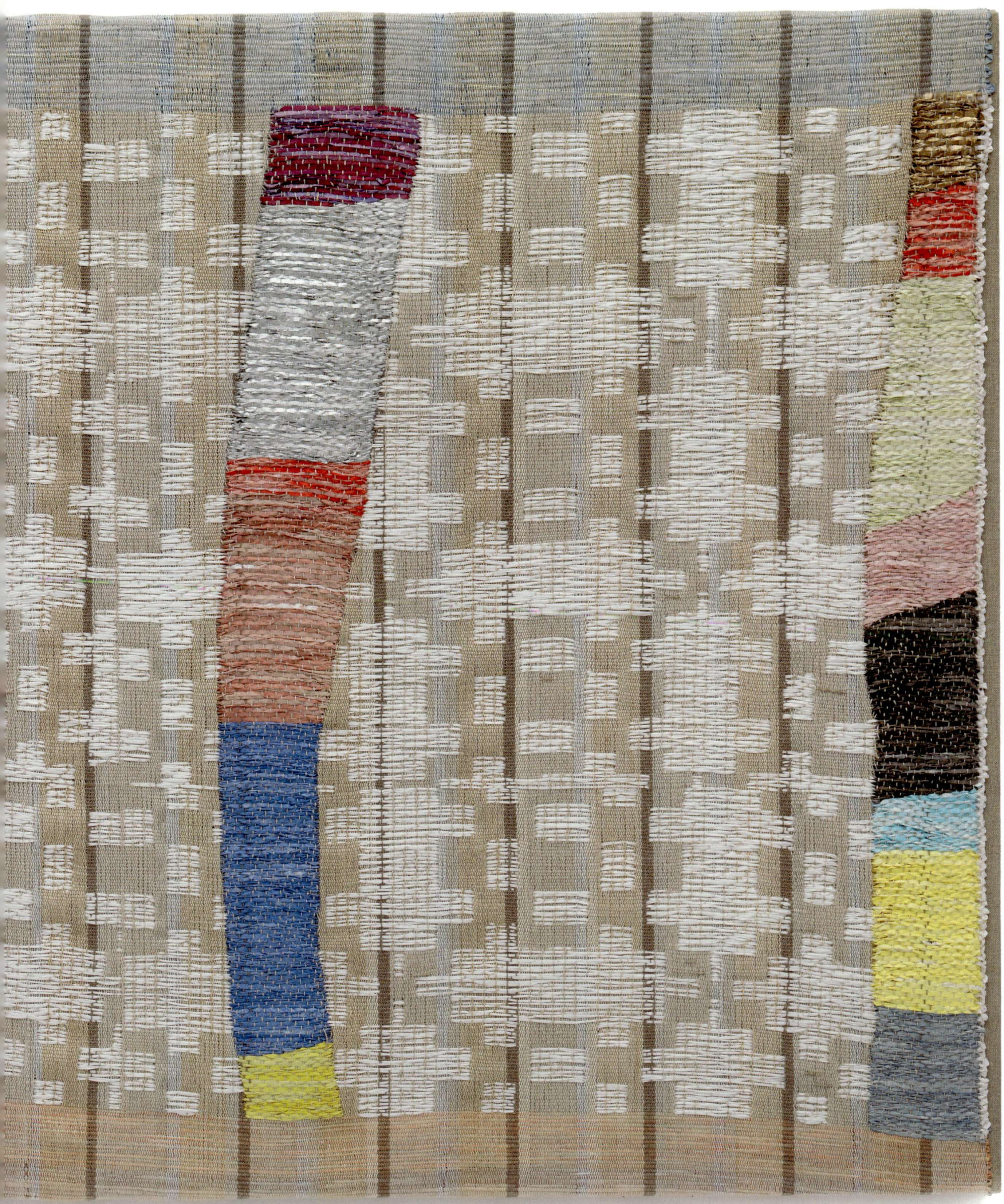

Fig. 10 Jacquard punched cards. Courtesy of Nicholas Gessler

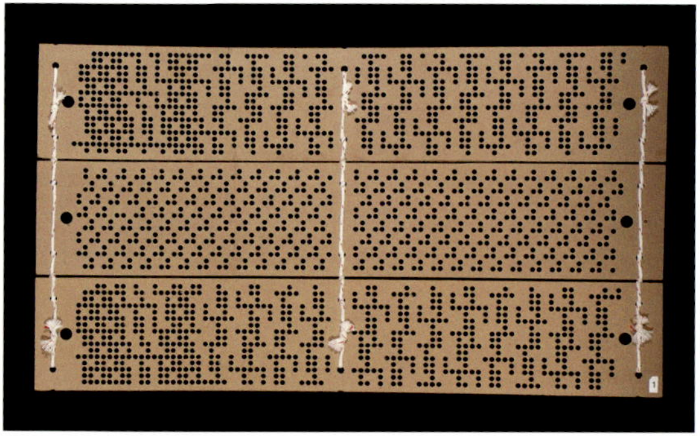

told me that the thing about weaving was that, unlike photography, where students might gather for a crit but then scatter to the winds, weaving required all the students to sit together in a room and work for hours at a loom, and in this way a community gets built. This is one story of how to be a fiber artist, and then Matson gave it all up. She moved to Southern California and dedicated herself to working alone every day on a mechanized Jacquard loom. The rarity of the loom alone sets her apart from contemporaries, but considering Jacquard as a degree of difficulty removed from weaving on the handloom or a backstrap loom (which mostly produces what is known in the industry as "plain cloth" or "double-faced fabrics") is to compare, perhaps, walking to dancing. Matson is decidedly not "taking a thread for a walk," as Albers once famously said of weaving, but choreographing a troupe of more than eight hundred individually moving parts. The Jacquard loom was first developed at the behest of Napoleon in order to make highly decorated silks—"fancy fabrics," that's the technical term, Matson says—on an industrial scale, and enough of these intensely wrought show-offs to decorate palaces. In seeking to fulfill a demand for luxury, the eponymous Jacquard also inadvertently developed an early computer, the nineteenth-century system of punch cards that would become the progenitor of modern computation (fig. 10). When Matson prepares to make a piece on the Jacquard loom, she must first code it with a sequence of black and white squares, a binary system predating zeroes and ones that instructs a machine to perform a series of replicable, automated tasks.

To say that Matson works from sight, then, is to fall short: she works from vision. When she shows me her preliminary programming for a piece, I cannot understand which completed artwork I am seeing on her computer screen. The code looks nothing at all like the weaving that results from it, a translation we accept daily in our use of interfaces that derive also from code, but a process we confront much less casually in art, and certainly even less in a medium shaded so heavily with the romanticism of handcraft. What modern Jacquard looms do particularly well is make weavings that look like photographs—family portraits on throw blankets are particularly popular—the image scanned into the computer and then replicated. Instead, Matson makes extravagant use of this industrial process, in both time and result. She harnesses the intricacy, and then undermines it, "intentionally finding ways of working that will make it less dexterous," she says. Each "pixel" of her images is a separate weave structure, broken down into still more granular code. What we see as shadow, what we see as something receding or sitting on top of the image plane, is not a shadow, not a string pulled taut to breaking, but a different weave, and theoretically with an infinite number more possible—she programs a draft pattern for me as I watch and names it "Su." Of the thousands of draft patterns she has made and saved, the maximum she can use at any one time is 255. Matson might spend as much time programming the Jacquard loom as she spends weaving each piece in concert with the machine: weeks to set up the process and weeks more of standing while passing the weft, only to create an artwork of deceptive simplicity that looks, say, like a gestural wash of brushstrokes. In *Untitled (Rose, Aquamarine, Amber)*, a triptych from a series begun in 2016, Matson and her loom weave what appear to be layers of thin pigment wash, with overlapping edges (fig. 11). Our perception of color sharpens visually within a limited palette, a heightened response to slight gradations. But in Matson's work, the tonal change is not an actual change in the color of the material. The pigments do not mix where the strokes overlap; the ink does not become more saturated. The thread stays the same color throughout. It is only, simply, a change in how we see the color, from how much of the thread is brought to the surface by Matson's choice of weave structure. A weaving is also an illusion.

Across series of works, an idea that Matson embraces is a certain light effortlessness of image, even a disarming slightness in a deliberate embrace of archetypes of beauty. She is fascinated by flowers, with the range of representations of this idealized concept that somehow, in their diverse simplifications, all read as "flower." The fat-petaled daisy, the single protea—it is an icon that appears often in her work, this image at once enduring and antimonumental, and a nod to her longstanding engagement with the ecological and spiritual wonder to be had in the hard-won but fleeting, the "immediacy in a laborious process," as she says. How something as diminutive, as pretty as a bloom sits against the long stretch of incremental effort required to render it is a driving question of Matson's work, and perhaps gets at her relationship to her obtuse method. Weaving is a time-based process, it is often said, with surrender to a meditative pace, a practice in patience. What Matson conveys within this expenditure is a moment: a dissolving field of color, a brushstroke, a view, a flower. We are inconsequential when faced with the immensity of time, she tells me, and we know this as deeply as we know its opposite—that we must nonetheless live as though we believe this effort matters. Matson has spent decades developing an untransferable specialized knowledge, at the synthesis of something made by hand and something formed by a machine. Each piece requires dozens of hours to complete, and she cannot hold the piece off the loom and approbate it until it is done—and she didn't even like weaving the first time she tried it. She thought, *This is it?* Then she tried Jacquard, which takes even longer. "I'm a slow burn," Matson says. (This mirrors Albers's initial reaction to the medium as well: "I thought

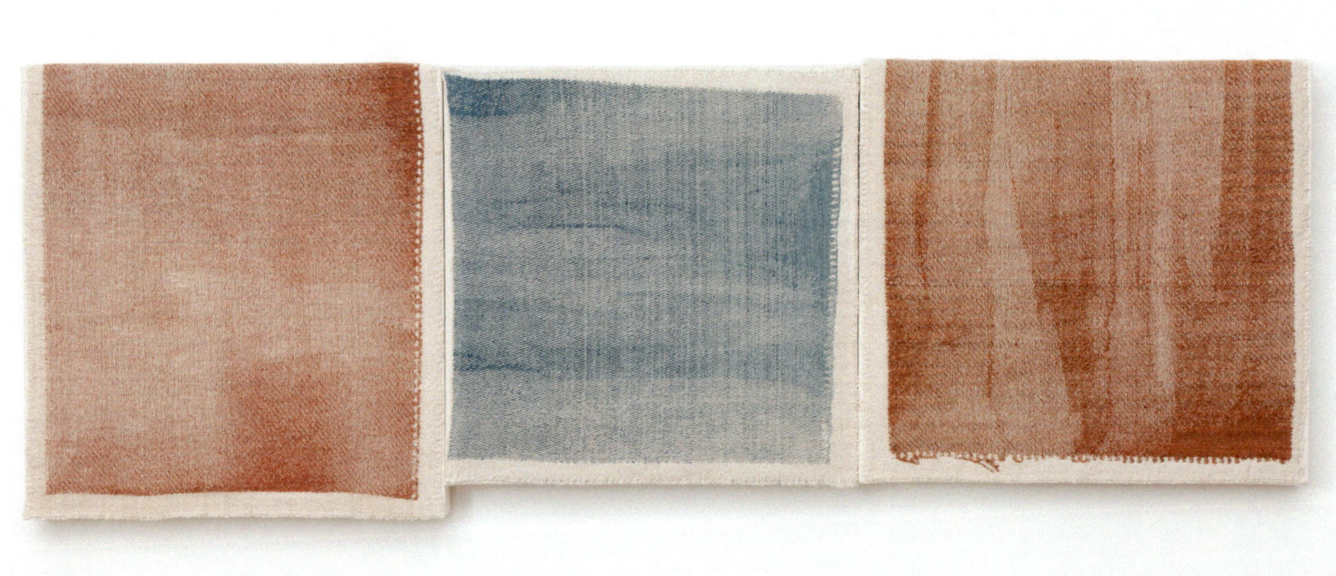

Fig. 11 Christy Matson, *Untitled (Rose, Aquamarine, Amber)*, 2016. Alpaca, naturally dyed wool, 21½ × 60 in. Courtesy of the artist and Volume Gallery, Chicago

[weaving] was rather sissy," she recalled later in an interview. "Just these threads."[4])

Yet in just these threads we confront the "basic idea about how things transform," Matson says. The yarns become cloth, the time becomes a dedication. But the actual matter is unaltered by the effort in weaving—not burned, not hardened, not less nor more. And in this way weaving comes very close to the idea of magic, or at least a "magical quality," Matson says, in which what transforms is not the material itself but our capacity to experience the world simultaneously as a real world, as real as we will ever have, and as a world of contradictory belief, of perspectives we cannot fully know and extrasensory perception, as the philosopher David Abram wrote in *The Spell of the Sensuous*:

The mutual inscription of others in my experience, and (as I must assume) of myself in their experiences, effects the interweaving of our individual phenomenal fields into a single, ever-shifting fabric, *a single phenomenal world or "reality."*[5]

It is getting hot in the studio. I gather my things and prepare to leave, and ask Matson about the rest of her afternoon, this sunny day in Los Angeles. She tells me she will spend it alone in this room undoing a section of her latest piece, where a spray-painted silver fiber did not do what she had hoped it would do. And I think suddenly but do not say then that maybe this is the truest thing about weaving, at least if one recalls the story of Penelope, unraveling and remaking the same piece of cloth daily as an assertion of her independence, to keep those pushy suitors at bay. Of the sheer tenacity and commitment it takes to work in fiber, where there is no shortcut, "life is a metaphor for weaving," Matson says. The action of weaving is indistinguishable from the action of unweaving: the same motion, the same hand, the same long threads of time.

Notes

1. Jennifer Licht, "An Interview with Dorothea Rockburne," *Artforum* 12, no. 6 (March 1972): 36.

2. Lisa Nakamura, "Indigenous Circuits: Navajo Women and the Racialization of Early Electronic Manufacture," *American Quarterly* 66, no. 4 (December 2014): 919–41.

3. Donna J. Haraway, "A Manifesto for Cyborgs: Science, Technology, and Socialist Feminism in the 1980s," *Socialist Review* 15, no. 2 (1985): 65–107.

4. Charles Darwent, "Weaving Walls: How Anni Albers Challenged Bauhaus Prejudice," *Art Newspaper*, October 7, 2018, https://www.theartnewspaper.com/feature/weaving-walls-how-anni-albers-challenged-bauhaus-prejudice.

5. David Abram, *The Spell of the Sensuous* (New York: Vintage Books, 1996), 39. Emphasis mine.

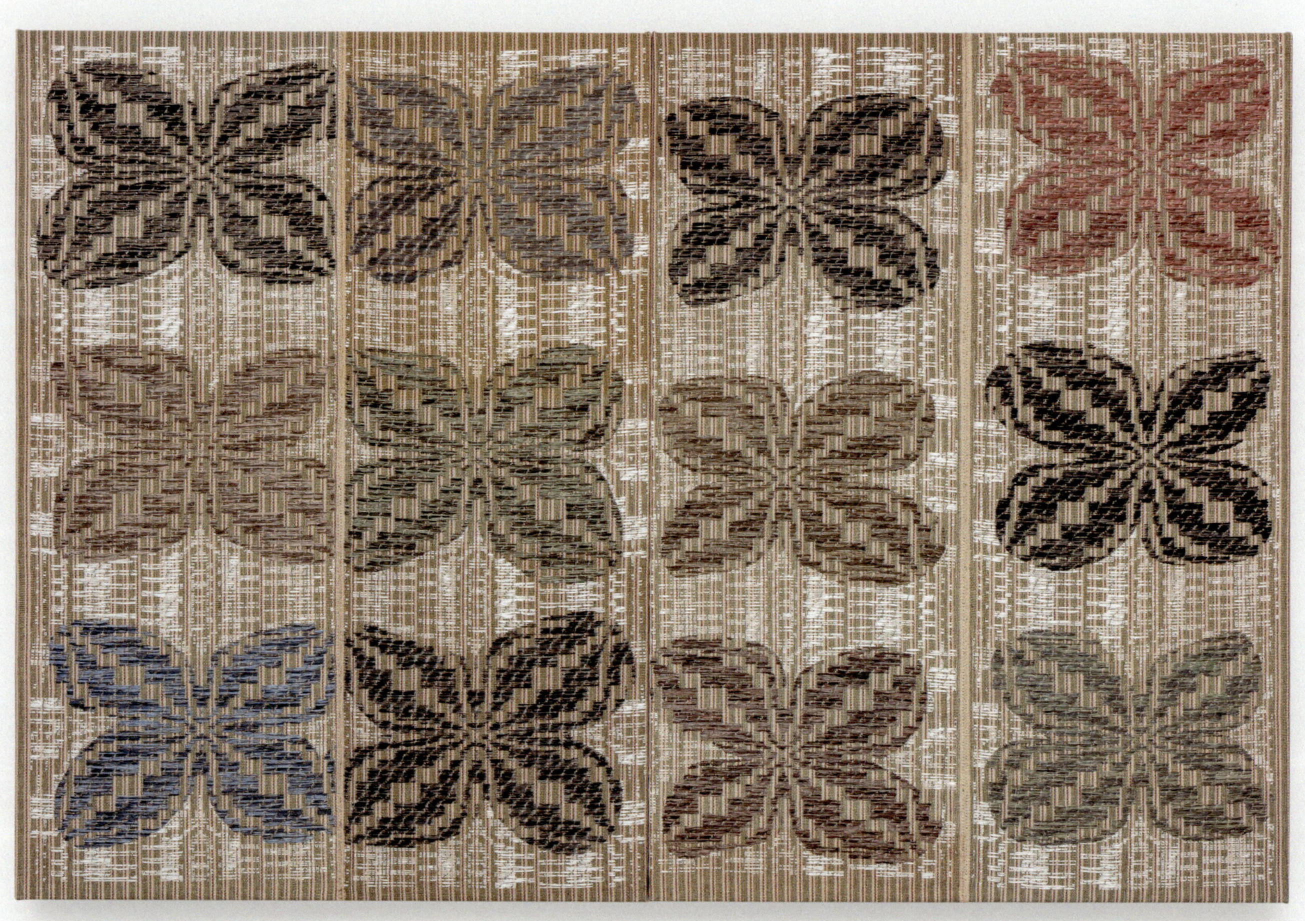

Flowering Dogwood Variation, 2020

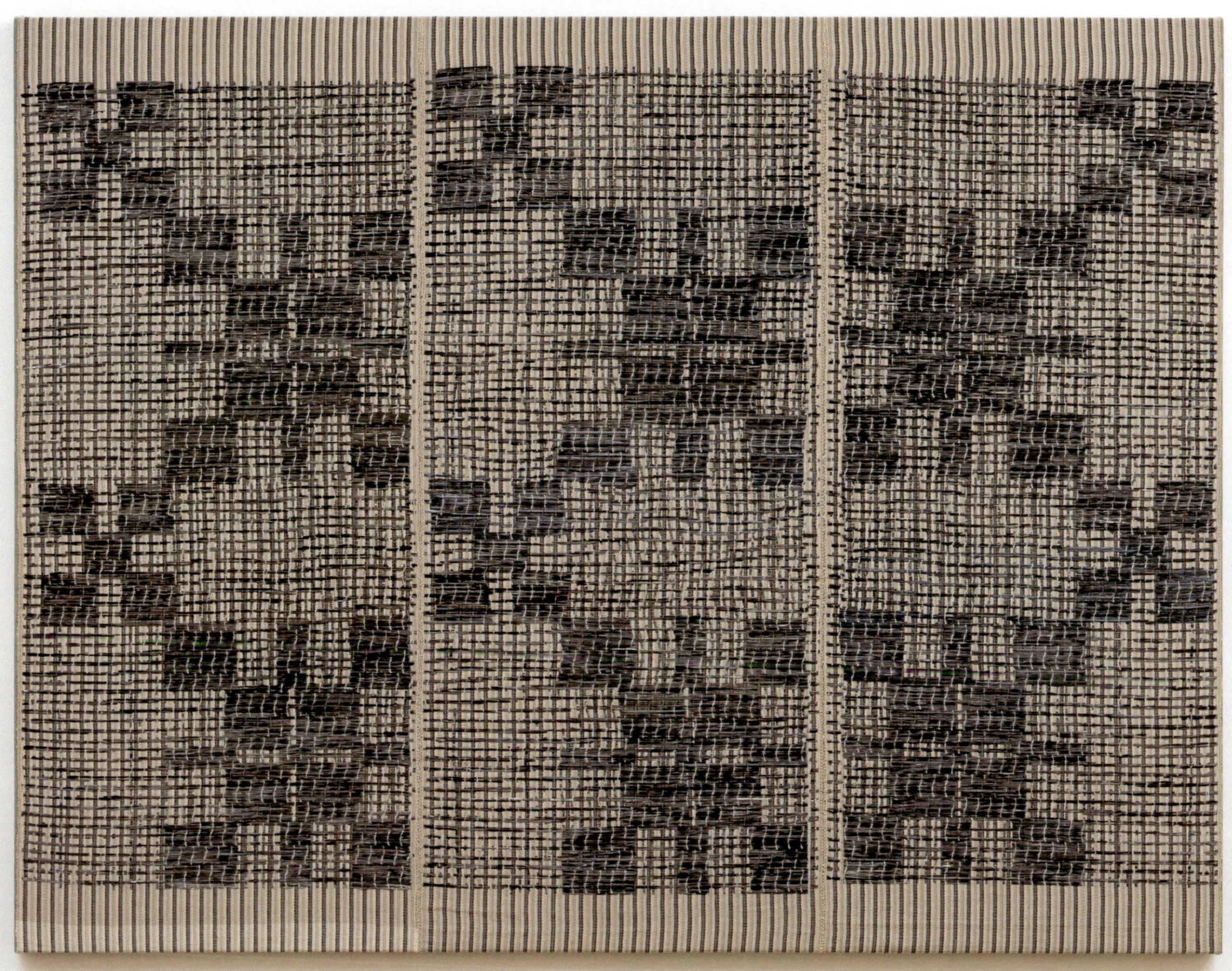

Overshot Grid Variation, 2019

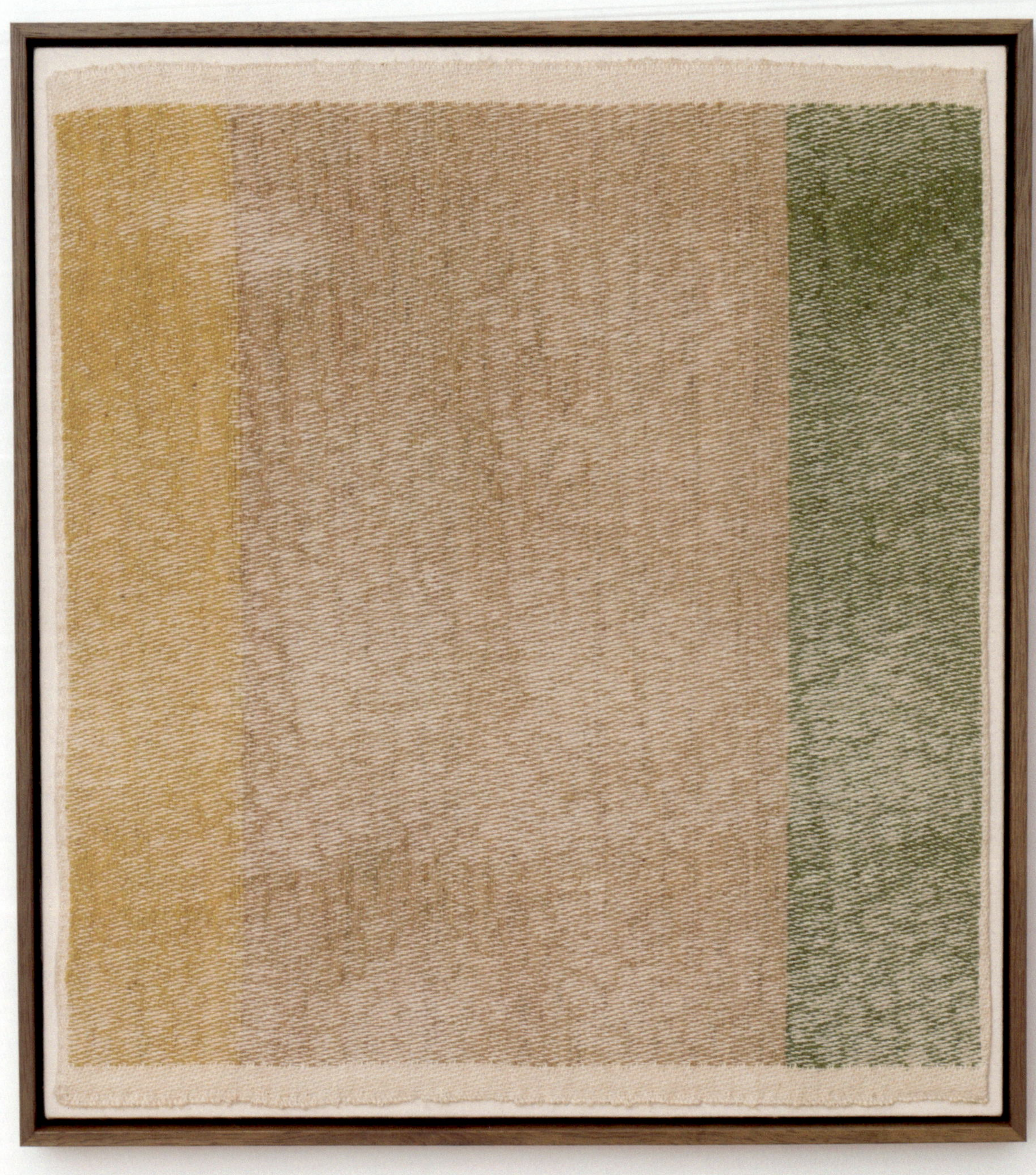

Wattle, 2016

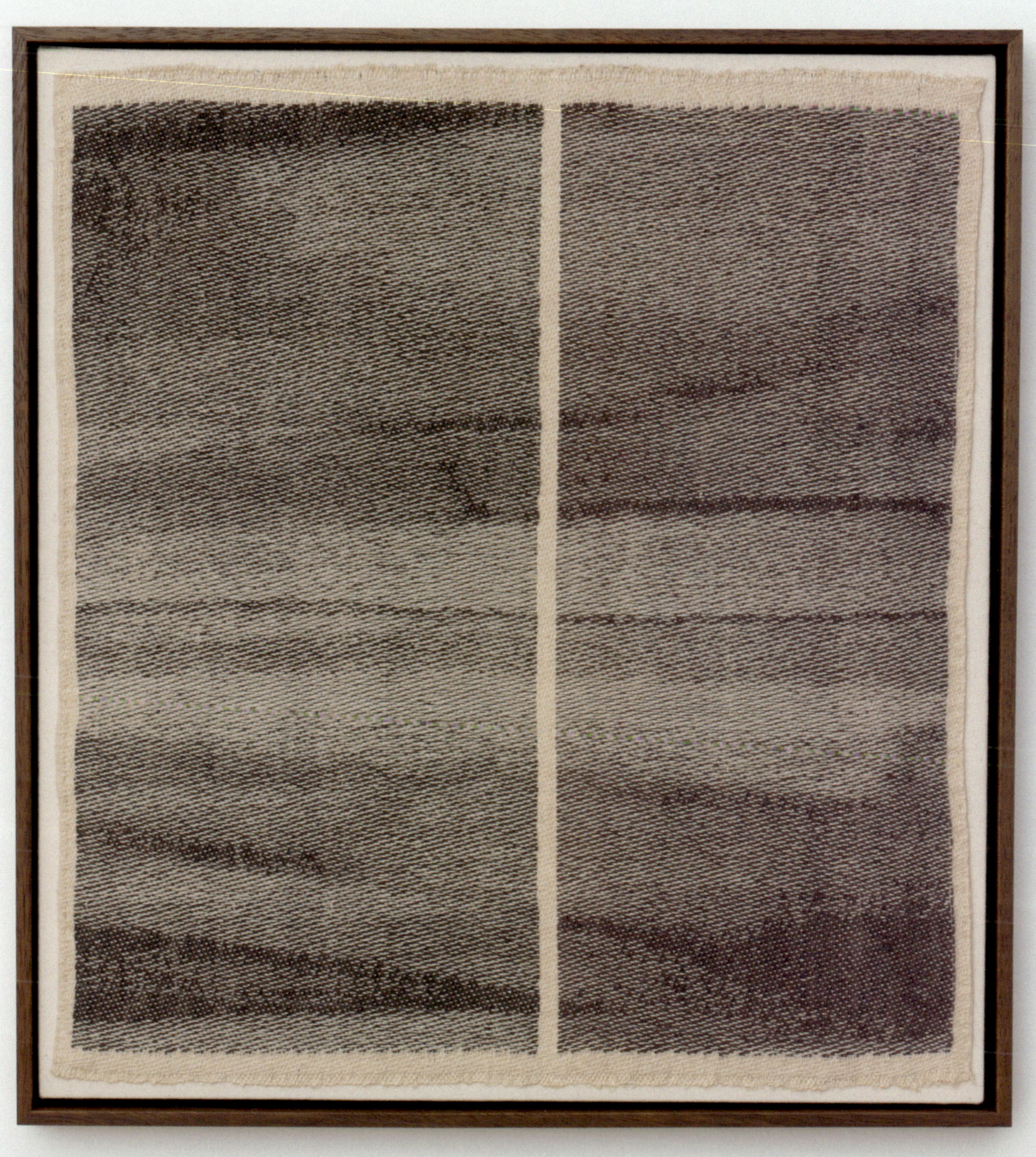

Wyo, 2016

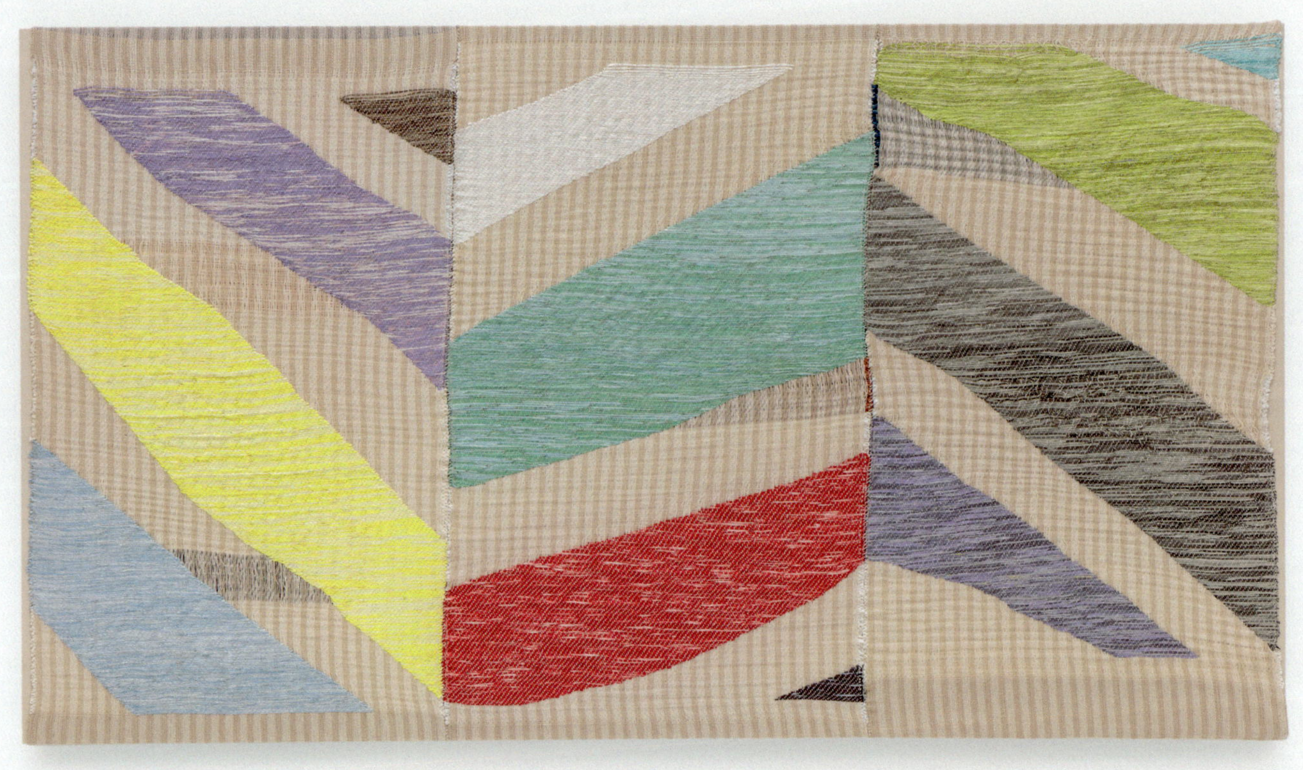

Untitled (Winding I), 2019

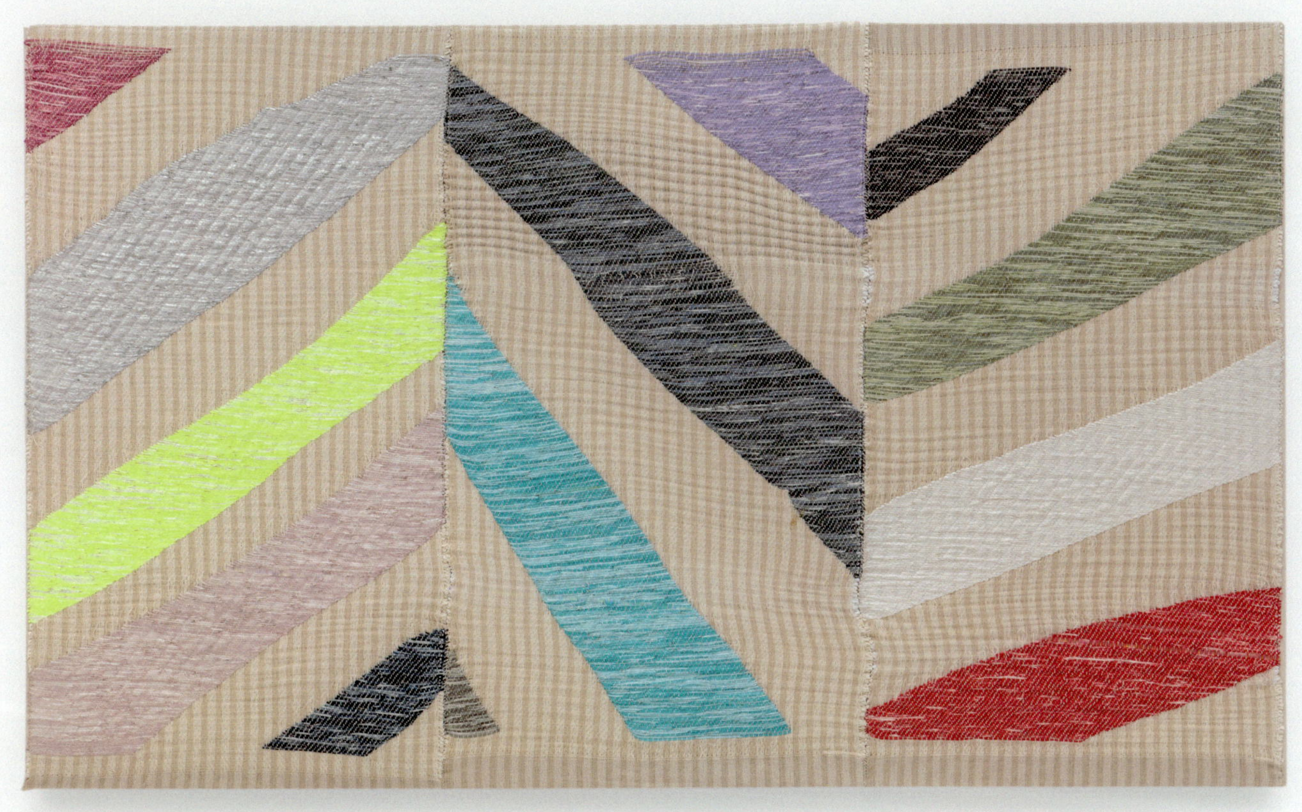

Untitled (Winding II), 2019

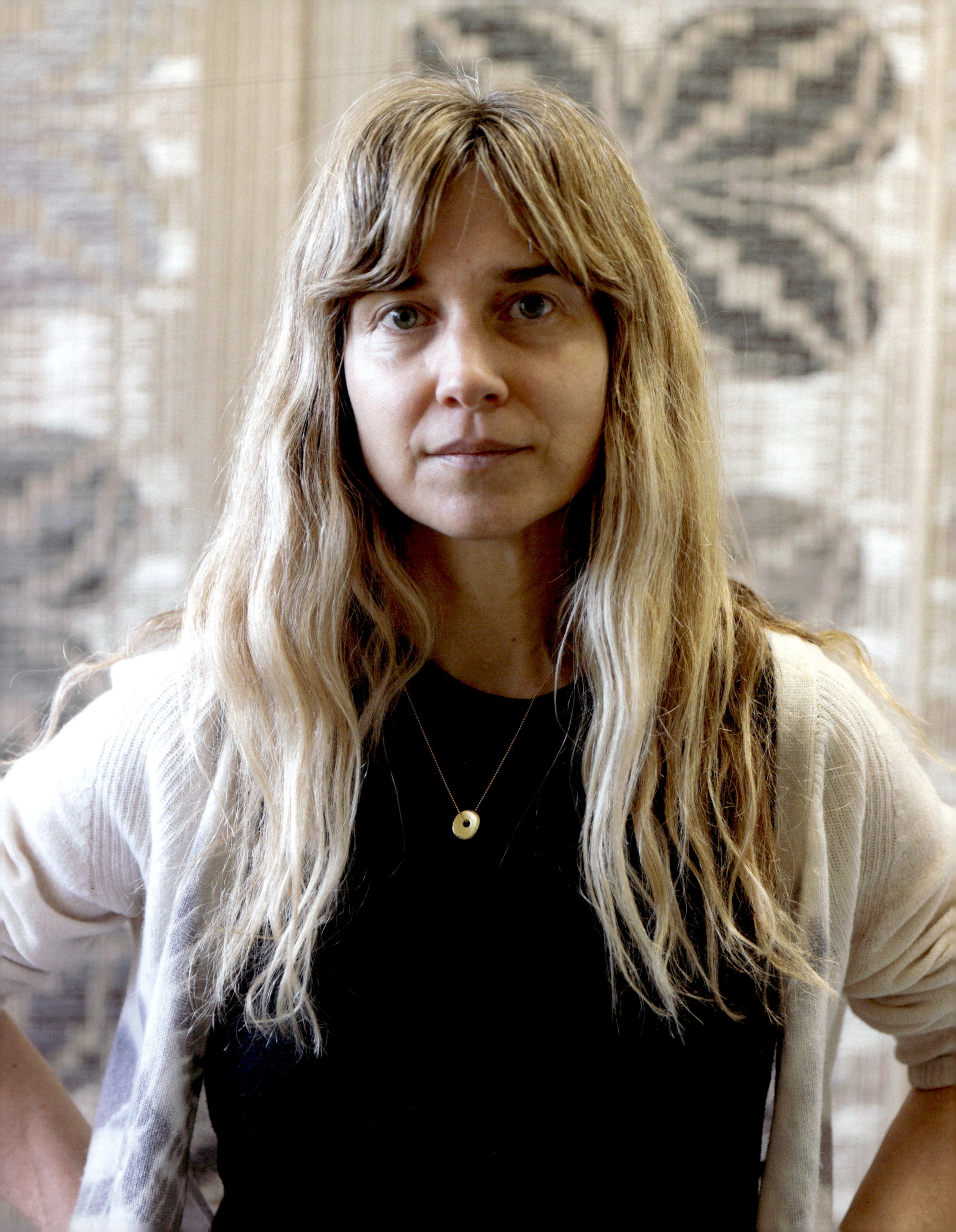

Conversation with Christy Matson

Monica Obniski

Monica Obniski Let's start at the beginning. What did you want to be when you grew up?

Christy Matson When I was growing up I wanted to be a psychologist. Actually, I was just thinking about this recently.... What a strange thought! I guess what attracted me to the profession, as a child, was the idea of sitting and talking, listening to people. Thinking about this today, I wanted to effect positive change in people.

In many ways, this impetus is not that dissimilar from being an art professor, so I guess I stumbled into the right profession! When I was teaching at the School of the Art Institute [SAIC], in the Fiber and Material Studies department, my teaching centered on listening to my students, and then pointing out ways that they could improve their projects. I was always striving to effect a positive outcome for my students. Actually, now that we've started talking about it, I miss teaching, but in the spirit of "know thyself," I know that I am good at doing two things at one time. Because there is a tremendous amount of emotional labor, which is invisible and unnoticed, devoted to being a professor, when the prospect of being a professor, an artist, and a mother materialized, well, I know myself well enough to know I can do two things well, but not three—and it's not fair. It wouldn't have been fair to my practice or my students.

MO Well, I'm glad that we don't have to use psychoanalysis in this interview! When did you become interested in making art?

CM While I was an undergraduate at the University of Washington. Growing up, we didn't go to museums and we didn't do "art stuff" as a family.... As opposed to now: I'm married to an artist and we spend much of our "free time" as a family attending exhibitions, traveling to see specific museum shows and biennials around the world. Its what we love to do. If you asked my daughter at age three who her favorite artist was she'd tell you John Baldessari and then describe his 1972 video where he attempts to teach the alphabet to a houseplant. When I was growing up, Seattle had limited access to contemporary art, so I didn't really see much of it. However, there was a wealth of local Native American art, especially if we think about a crossover between functional objects and art—such as baskets as a type of art.

MO Even though you are talking about Indigenous baskets, the Ed Rossbach enthusiast in me rejoices.

CM Well, you know he graduated from and taught at the University of Washington—my alma mater—for a few years. I started in UW's School of Art as a sophomore, when I began as a fiber major.

MO So you found your chosen medium of textiles during your second year of college. How did that happen?

CM Well, I started school as a drama major, then took a leave of absence, traveling to Nepal for three months. After I returned, I cut through the School of Art on a rainy day, and the building just had a different aura. I paused at a bulletin board that described some courses that included natural dyeing, weaving, et cetera, and all of these things sounded so interesting. Actually, the University of Washington's fiber department used to be a home economics department.

MO Right, similar to the University of Wisconsin–Madison's School of Human Ecology, where textiles are a major, and where you did a residency.

CM Precisely. What is also rather remarkable is that my grandmother studied home economics at the University of Washington in 1936. Of course, at that time, there were very few avenues for women to study at university, and this was one of the accepted routes. It's quite funny, but actually, before I even started weaving on the University's floor looms, I bought a loom—because somehow I knew that this was my path—the Leclerc Nilus Low Castle 4 Harness Floor Loom. Unfortunately, it was overly technical, and it felt too limiting to me.

MO Okay, so you graduate from the University of Washington, with a solid education in handweaving on floor looms, which you have intimated was not really your thing. How did the adventure continue?

CM I went to North Carolina. At the invitation of University of Washington professor Layne Goldsmith, I was able to go to North Carolina to obtain some additional training. As a Capricorn, I am a practical-minded person, so I just kept

Fig. 12 Pages from William Watson's *Advanced Textile Design* (London: Longmans, Green and Co., 1913). University of California, Berkeley Libraries

(Overleaf) *Magical Thinking*, 2020

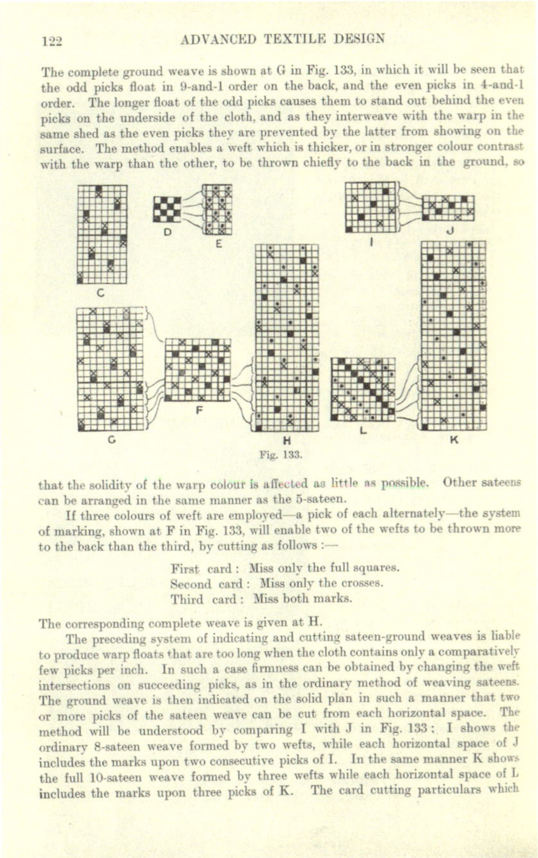

122 ADVANCED TEXTILE DESIGN

The complete ground weave is shown at G in Fig. 133, in which it will be seen that the odd picks float in 9-and-1 order on the back, and the even picks in 4-and-1 order. The longer float of the odd picks causes them to stand out behind the even picks on the underside of the cloth, and as they interweave with the warp in the same shed as the even picks they are prevented by the latter from showing on the surface. The method enables a weft which is thicker, or in stronger colour contrast with the warp than the other, to be thrown chiefly to the back in the ground, so

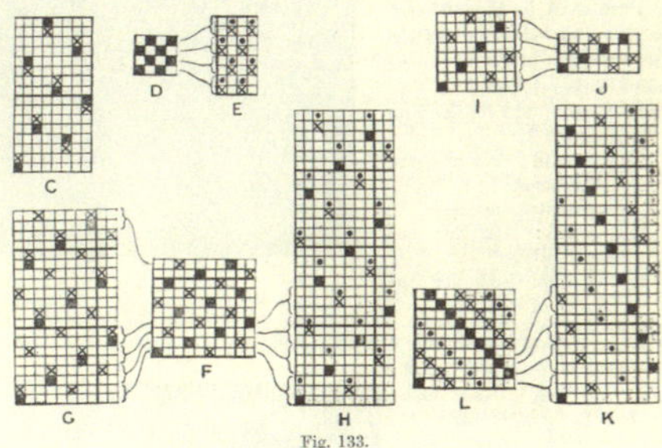

Fig. 133.

that the solidity of the warp colour is affected as little as possible. Other sateens can be arranged in the same manner as the 5-sateen.

If three colours of weft are employed—a pick of each alternately—the system of marking, shown at F in Fig. 133, will enable two of the wefts to be thrown more to the back than the third, by cutting as follows :—

First card : Miss only the full squares.
Second card : Miss only the crosses.
Third card : Miss both marks.

The corresponding complete weave is given at H.

The preceding system of indicating and cutting sateen-ground weaves is liable to produce warp floats that are too long when the cloth contains only a comparatively few picks per inch. In such a case firmness can be obtained by changing the weft intersections on succeeding picks, as in the ordinary method of weaving sateens. The ground weave is then indicated on the solid plan in such a manner that two or more picks of the sateen weave can be cut from each horizontal space. The method will be understood by comparing I with J in Fig. 133 : I shows the ordinary 8-sateen weave formed by two wefts, while each horizontal space of J includes the marks upon two consecutive picks of I. In the same manner K shows the full 10-sateen weave formed by three wefts while each horizontal space of L includes the marks upon three picks of K. The card cutting particulars which

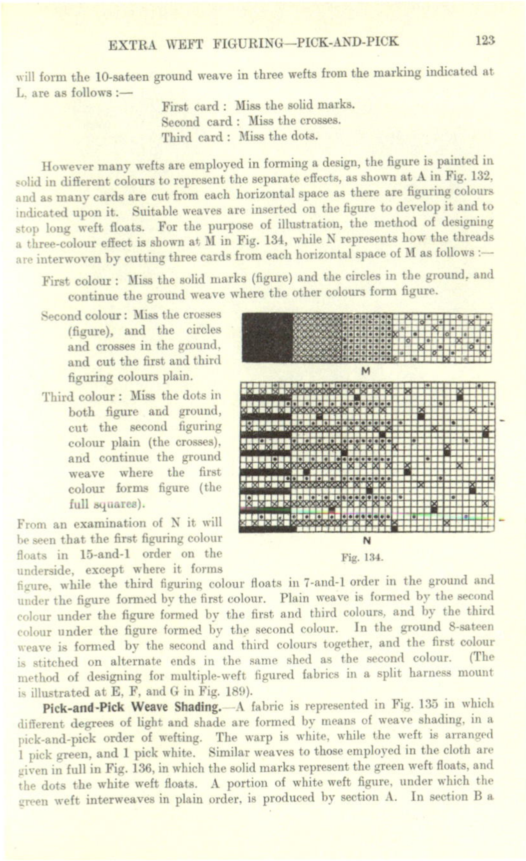

EXTRA WEFT FIGURING—PICK-AND-PICK 123

will form the 10-sateen ground weave in three wefts from the marking indicated at L, are as follows :—

First card : Miss the solid marks.
Second card : Miss the crosses.
Third card : Miss the dots.

However many wefts are employed in forming a design, the figure is painted in solid in different colours to represent the separate effects, as shown at A in Fig. 132, and as many cards are cut from each horizontal space as there are figuring colours indicated upon it. Suitable weaves are inserted on the figure to develop it and to stop long weft floats. For the purpose of illustration, the method of designing a three-colour effect is shown at M in Fig. 134, while N represents how the threads are interwoven by cutting three cards from each horizontal space of M as follows :—

First colour : Miss the solid marks (figure) and the circles in the ground, and continue the ground weave where the other colours form figure.

Second colour : Miss the crosses (figure), and the circles and crosses in the ground, and cut the first and third figuring colours plain.

Third colour : Miss the dots in both figure and ground, cut the second figuring colour plain (the crosses), and continue the ground weave where the first colour forms figure (the full squares).

M

N

Fig. 134.

From an examination of N it will be seen that the first figuring colour floats in 15-and-1 order on the underside, except where it forms figure, while the third figuring colour floats in 7-and-1 order in the ground and under the figure formed by the first colour. Plain weave is formed by the second colour under the figure formed by the first and third colours, and by the third colour under the figure formed by the second colour. In the ground 8-sateen weave is formed by the second and third colours together, and the first colour is stitched on alternate ends in the same shed as the second colour. (The method of designing for multiple-weft figured fabrics in a split harness mount is illustrated at E, F, and G in Fig. 189).

Pick-and-Pick Weave Shading.—A fabric is represented in Fig. 135 in which different degrees of light and shade are formed by means of weave shading, in a pick-and-pick order of wefting. The warp is white, while the weft is arranged 1 pick green, and 1 pick white. Similar weaves to those employed in the cloth are given in full in Fig. 136, in which the solid marks represent the green weft floats, and the dots the white weft floats. A portion of white weft figure, under which the green weft interweaves in plain order, is produced by section A. In section B a

thinking that I needed to get a job, and with a fiber degree I could be a textile designer. I then trained on textile-specific software that made it possible to weave anything I want—and it was a revelation: imagery and structure were combined.

The class that I took was at The Jacquard Center in Hendersonville, North Carolina, where we lived and worked for two weeks. While there, I spent a lot of time in front of files on a Mac computer, and it was really a deep dive into structure. In those days, William Watson's *Advanced Textile Design* (fig. 12), as interpreted by our instructor Bethanne Knudson, was my guiding light. In fact, she redrew all of the draft illustrations by hand so that she would not be in copyright violation—amazing! Before Oriole Mill existed, Bethanne offered a mill-access class, which was one of the first to be offered in the country. She also took us to visit other mills in the South. After we made our files on the computer, Bethanne would load us into her car, and we'd drive to the mill to make the weavings.

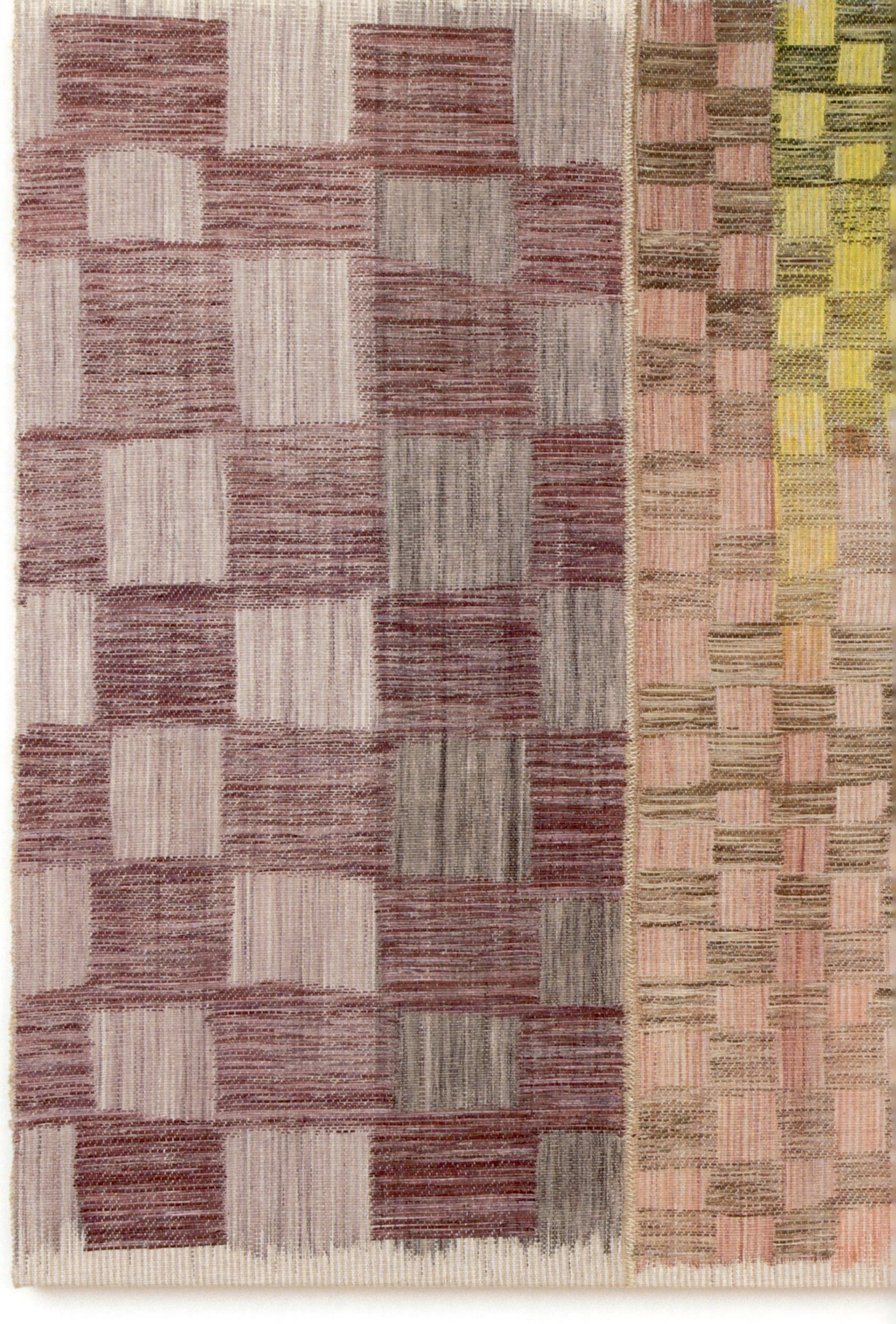

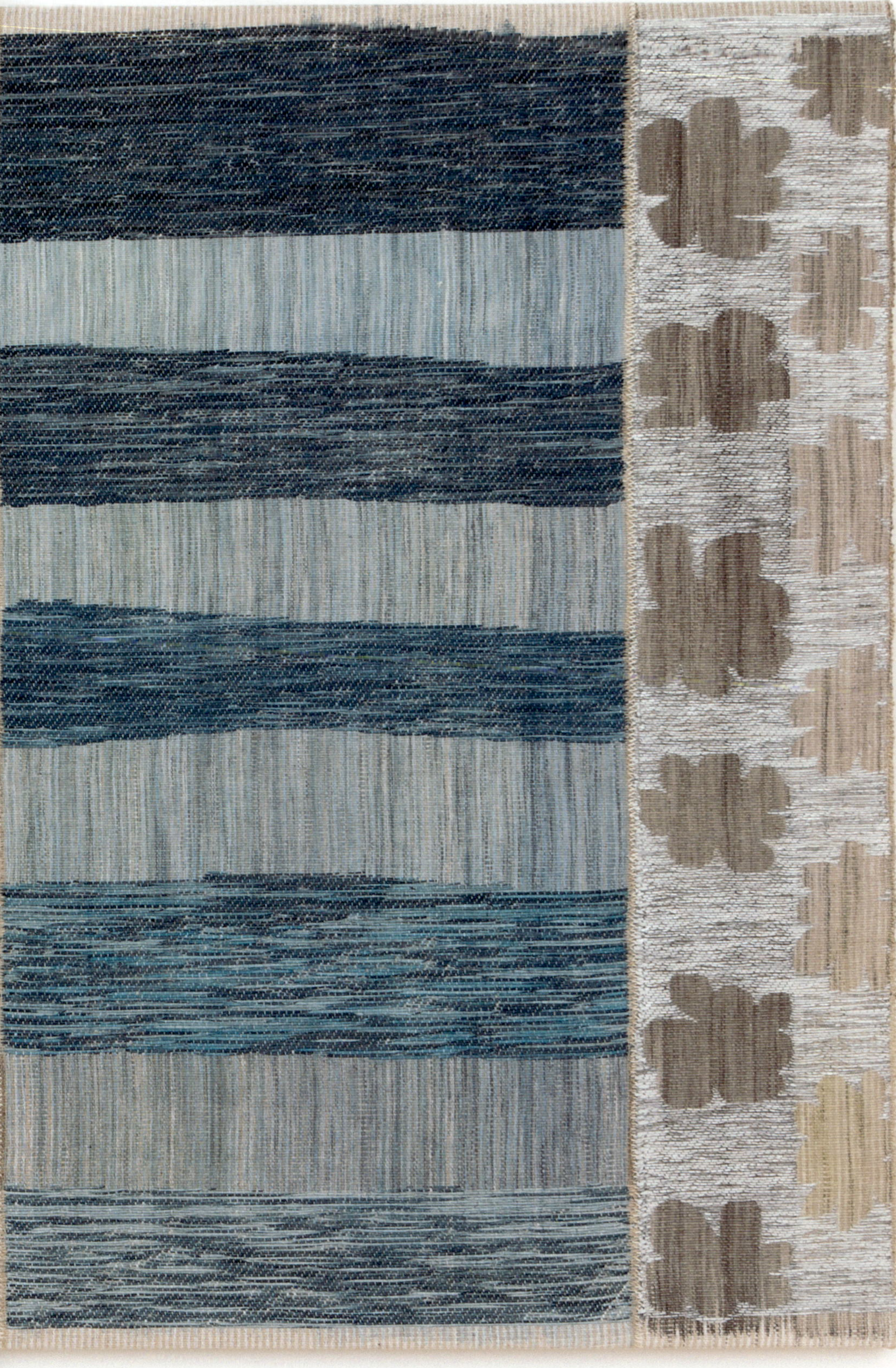

In Trion, North Carolina, at the Pure Country Mill, I witnessed a single-width repeat across the length of the loom, as this mill was making throws for the gift market. But this was a trying time economically, because mills were being closed. This was a huge loss in the southeastern United States.

MO Christy, who else was present for these magical two weeks of weaving?

CM Well, Cynthia Schira, who is an important figure in the history of American weaving but rather overlooked these days. She is the one who told me about Haystack, and made an introduction to Stuart Kestenbaum, which then led to teaching there and joining the board. And, of course, there was Lia Cook.

MO Yes, the textile guru Lia Cook, who eventually became your professor.

CM I was at a point in my life where I thought that I would go to the Rhode Island School of Design [RISD] to become a textile designer. You see, I wasn't aware of any real examples in contemporary art to understand how fiber existed more broadly in the world. When I met Lia that summer, she suggested that I enroll in an MFA program with an art focus. But I still didn't know for myself, and that fall I went to Cranbrook—and decided against applying there. It's an excellent school but the location was too isolated for me. I've only ever lived in cities! I did apply to RISD, interviewed in January, but when I walked out, I determined that it too was the wrong place—and that Lia was right. I pivoted and applied to the California College of the Arts, and studied with Lia in Oakland, where the fiber department is located. My time with her was foundational.

I learned everything from her—and, most importantly for me at this time, all the technical stuff. I learned how to take that technical information, which was basically rote memorization, and then apply it in new ways. This makes all the difference. She had been working since the 1970s, with Ed Rossbach and then in Sweden. Lia has an experimental approach that is rooted in history. Her work is ambitious and rigorous, and it was the ultimate model. I feel that the way that I work is informed by Lia Cook's example. She was also a full-time professor, an artist, and raised a son.

MO Whoa—the total package.

CM Yes. She also provided a much-needed mentor/student relationship, and we were interested in the same things. I ended up being her TA for two years straight, and I learned everything from her. When the opportunity to teach in SAIC's Fiber and Material Studies department became a reality, I imported Lia's pedagogical model to SAIC.

MO Okay, so you were shaped by the technical spirit of Lia's weavings, and perhaps also the craft of weaving. In several previous interviews, you have referenced the work of Richard Sennett, particularly his book *The Craftsman*, and this poetic idea of working within a space of intuition. Do you consider yourself a craftsperson?

CM That book came out when I was still teaching, and when it was published there was *so much* conversation about Sennett's ideas about "tacit knowledge"—or what you know through your fingertips versus a more standard cerebral-type knowledge. It's not something I think too much about these days, but I do like a lot of what he has to say about the role of expertise and learning through doing. If anything, I think about this book as a pedagogical tool. I refer to myself as an artist, not a craftsperson, because that language term feels hyperspecific; when I think about the word "craft" in relation to my practice, it's as a verb and not a noun.

MO Some writers have discussed the current moment that we are in as a transitioning phase. We've moved from hand-production to industrial-production and back to some fetishized handwork in the twentieth century, and now some makers, like you, are combining digital technologies with handwork. Is this the next evolutionary step?

CM I don't know. It's interesting because in the early 2000s, there was a lot of dialogue about this topic. In fact, my graduate thesis explored this idea of the hand and digital, arguing that thinking about these two forces in opposition is not useful. I think that the combination of digital and the hand offers an alternative, or a third way. It was from this intellectual space that I started experimenting with sound textiles, as an embodied experience or a kind of phenomenological approach—understanding our bodies in a physical space and the intimacy that one experiences with textiles.

A lot has changed since I finished graduate school, including a perceived fear of the digital. Actually, what we should be worried about is data collection and privacy!

MO Thinking about your work and craft makes me wonder what your relationship is with other artistic media.

CM Well, right now, it is not important to me to experiment in other media. When I was finishing up my textile MFA, I was making work that explored the intersection of textiles and technology—works like sound compositions and interactive installations, but these always had a textile component. More recently, I investigated slip-based porcelain for my 2018 show *Rock, Paper, Scissors* at the Long Beach Museum of Art, but all of those shapes came out of textiles as well. The slip-casts were all made from different types of cones and yarn holders that are typically thrown away after they've been used. Now they are made in cardboard or plastic, but my mother collected and amassed spools and bobbins made out of wood and metal. When she passed away I inherited them. I grew up with these objects in our kitchen but strangely had never taken notice of what they were until they became mine.

Sometimes I do have an urge to make something that isn't a textile, but actually I

Full Moon Forest, 2016

really just want to do this. It's interesting—because of the gendered nature of textiles, if I were a painter, you probably wouldn't ask me a question like this. But, this—a single-minded focus—is an old-fashioned approach to being a contemporary artist. I've been making textiles like this since it was a deeply unpopular medium, and I understand that fads come and go. Very likely ten years from now interest in textiles may have receded again.

MO Well, I don't know about that. I think your work is compelling and smart, which is why it is being actively collected and considered, but I am intrigued by this idea of the gendered nature of textiles and artistic value.

CM I think it is so interesting that the Whitney is showing craft alongside fine art in their recently opened exhibition *Making Knowing: Craft in Art, 1950–2019*. A friend recently texted me some of the didactic information from the show, and they are talking about marginalization, gender, power structures... finally. There is so much gender-based exclusion in the art world, particularly when one is making objects or using techniques that have been historically subjected to sexism and snobbery. I think shows like this are important to remind us all about how radical it was to be making work like this in the 1950s—and before that.

What if instead of aspiring to mimic the white male mainstream, we attach artistic value to other modes of creativity? I love that we are now asking questions surrounding this. Instead of agreeing that for your work to be valued, you must make *X*, why don't we look at the work that women have historically always done and say that there is value in this previously marginalized type of artistic production? This is critically important.

MO As a design historian and a curator who trained in the decorative arts, I especially admire your dedication to the field, which, unfortunately, often gets unfairly maligned. I'd like to think about textiles more globally, as they have been around for centuries. What aspects of global textile culture are found within your work?

CM I think, first and foremost, weave structures. Ideas of a global textile culture are apparent in the overshot techniques, but also in the waffle weaves that I create. I also incorporate satin weave structures, which have been associated with the South of France, in the early 1800s when the Jacquard loom was developed (see *Full Moon Forest*, facing page). Also, the strategy of achieving a larger surface of cloth by stitching sections together, as I do for my larger work because of the limits of the loom widths, has been found throughout global textile history, particularly when you look at textiles of a domestic scale.

But then there are the fibers that I choose—from naturally dyed rug wool from Nepal and the domestic mill ends, to the surplus paper that I inherited from Lia Cook—I think all of these are parts of a global textile culture (see *I've Been Near You, but You've*

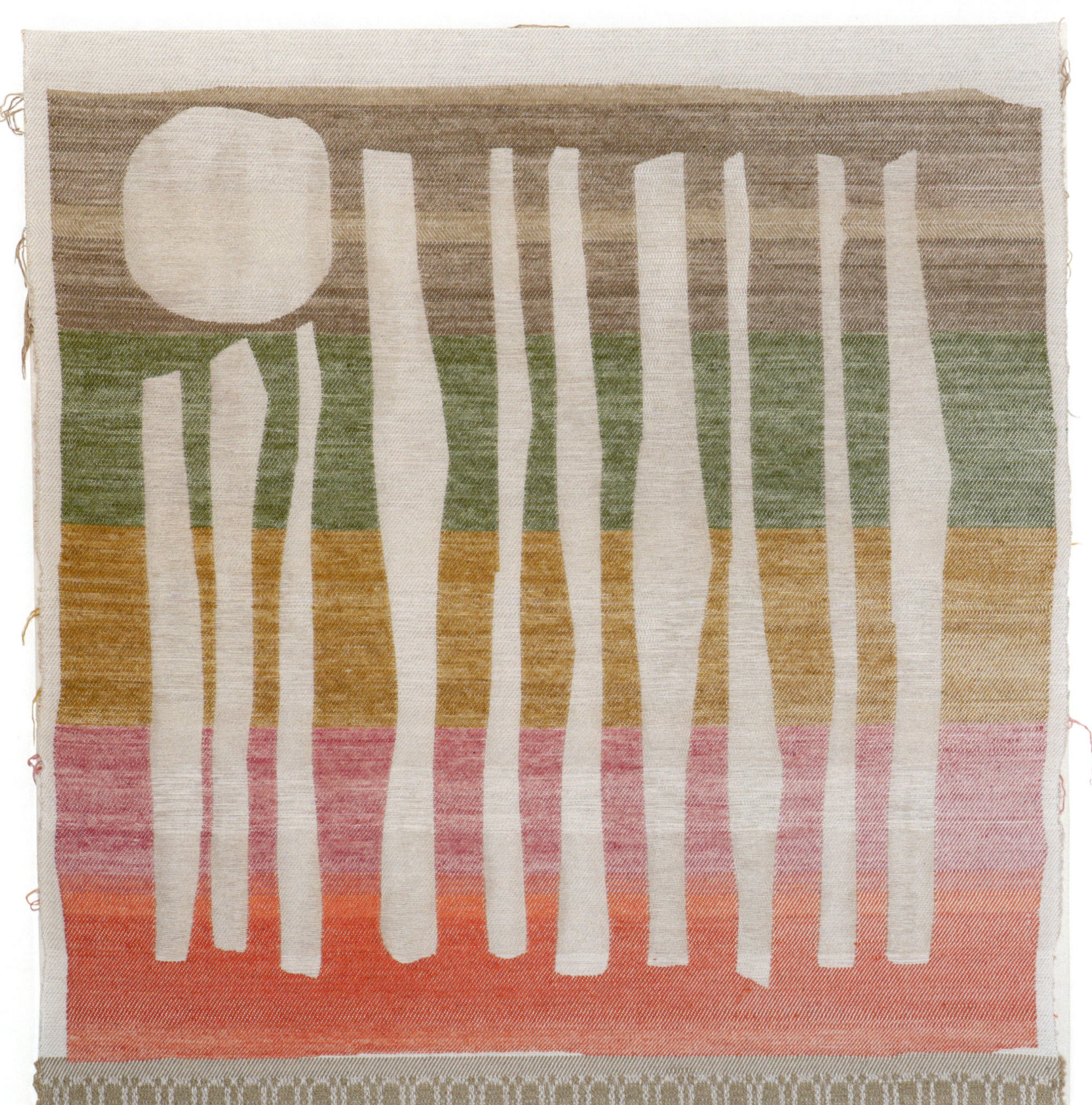

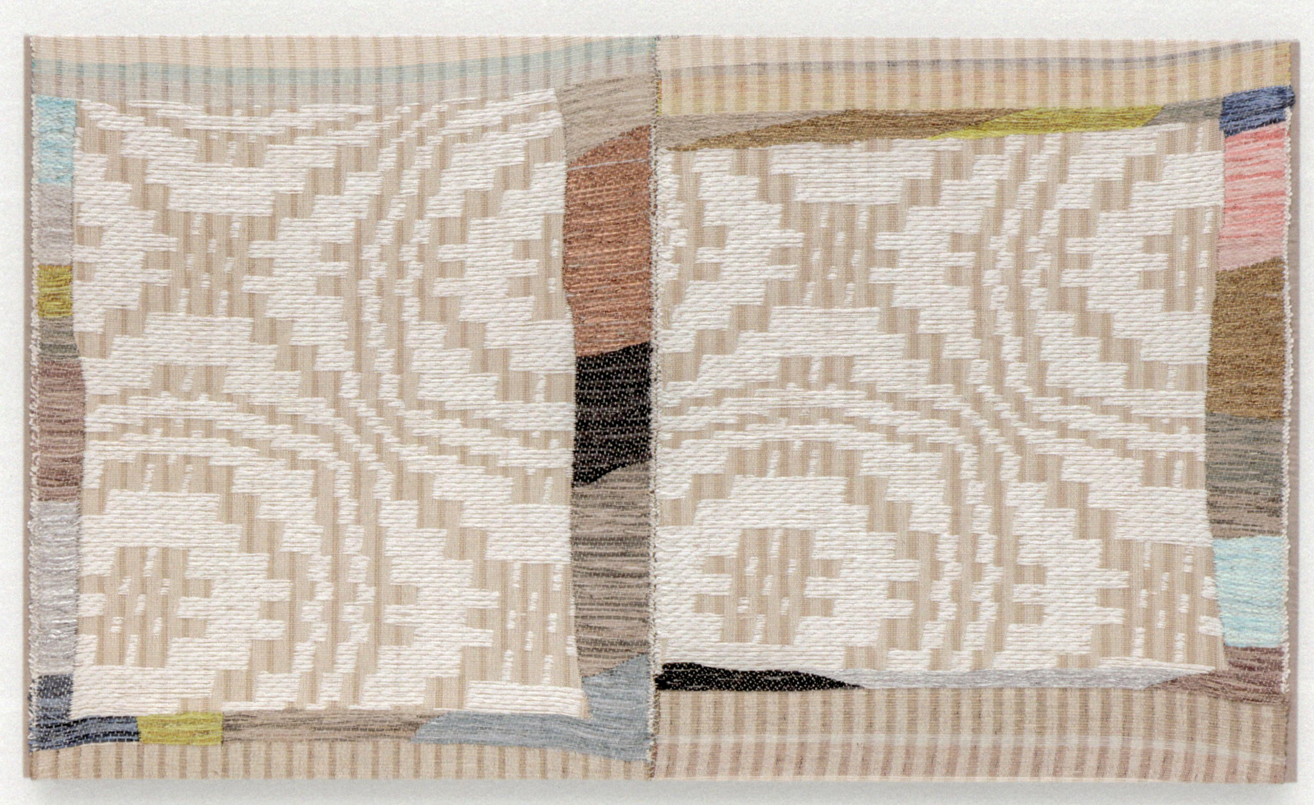

Overshot Variation 4, 2019/2020

Never Noticed Me, page 8). Further, we are living in a moment when what we are wearing comes from all parts of the world. In the same way, weave structures and materials are also from all over.

MO I'm loving this conversation because I feel like I am witnessing Professor Matson in action, especially when you discuss history.

CM Well, so much of my work is mining history. When you think about it, male artists have been mining history forever—think about someone like Picasso. When we reflect upon historical textiles, take the example of the triangle, a shape that is not specific to a particular region, or even overshot weaving, which can be found in the southeastern United States but also in Finland and Iran. This notion of simultaneity in textiles feels really remarkable because it underscores a level of ingenuity found within textiles over vast amounts of time and diverse places.

MO I want to shift to thinking about process: How do you start working on a new weaving? Analog sketching? Watercolor studies? When do you involve the computer?

CM It depends. I used to do more pen and ink sketches, but beginning in 2018 I developed a new way to work. I now go to books with different weave structures. So, for example, I took a photograph of an overshot structure, then I wove it as a picture of that structure. Something optical occurred when I figured out how to draft the overshot for a Jacquard. When weaving overshot as overshot, in other words, it is structurally overshot and visually, it is overshot as well... very meta, I know. I'm looking at self-reflexivity and thinking about reciprocity. In other words, the weaving looks like it does because it originated in itself (see *Untitled [Tabby]*, page 66), and I always use the structure to inform the direction that the weaving is going.

MO All right, but that is the structure. You then make choices about color, no?

CM Yes, I make subjective choices about color. I try not to overthink it.... It is a balance. It's interesting, sitting here, looking at what I have woven recently, it occurs to me that I need things to feel neutral, and then at other times, I need saturated, over-the-top color. Many of the colors that I use are a response to living and working in Los Angeles—these palm trees with gray skies, or the hot pink bougainvillea (see *Overshot Variation 3*, pages 42–43). Sometimes I use paper as the weft that I have painted, and I love the way that the material absorbs the paint, plus the telltale trace of the hand on the object. I used to work in my backyard, in a Quonset hut studio, and I was struck by the collision of urban and rural, as well as the drought conditions that are interrupted by shocks of color with flowers and jacaranda trees—these colors that defy expectations.

MO Lately, it seems like there are more makers experimenting with the TC2 loom—your tool of

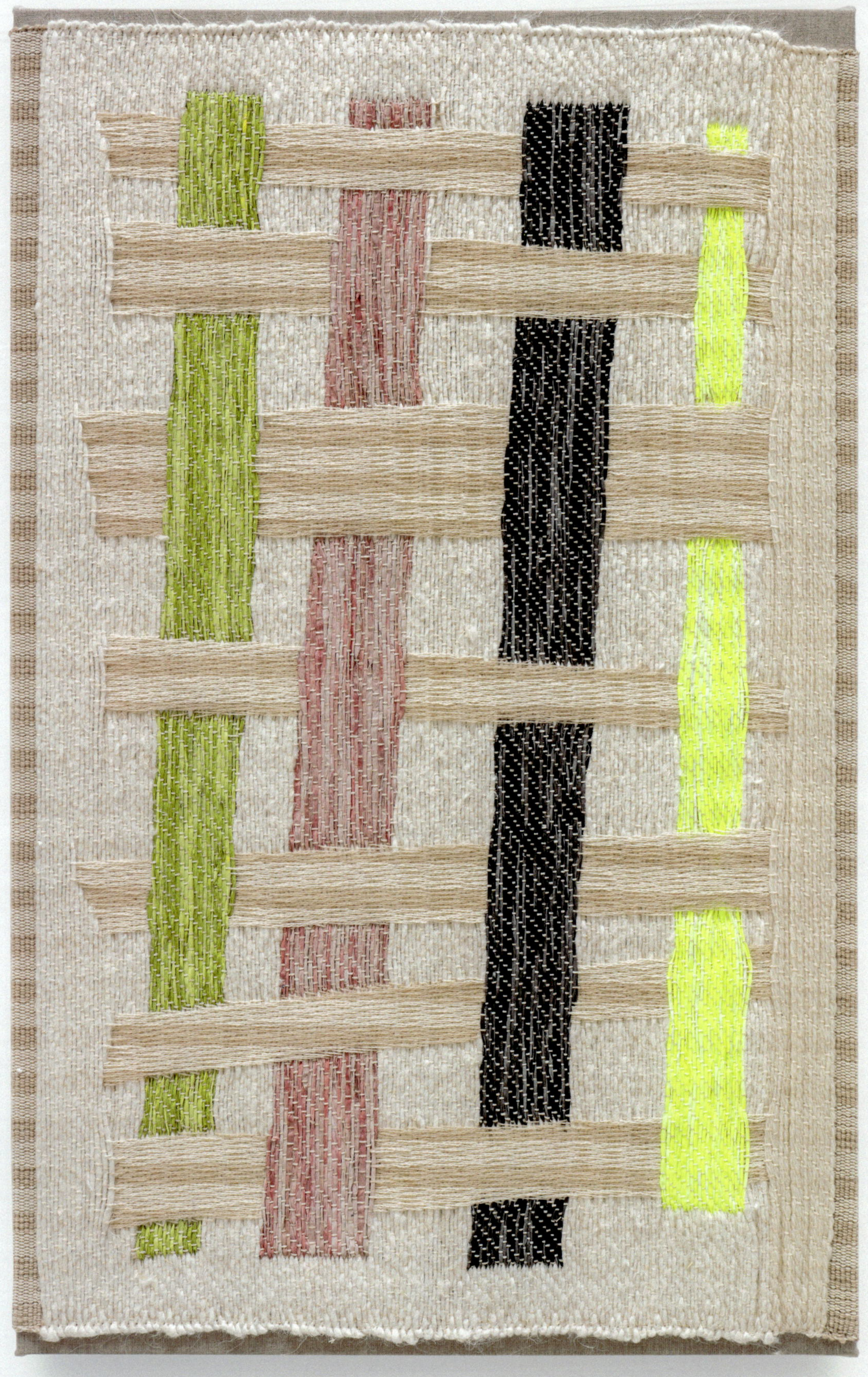

Untitled (Tabby), 2019

choice. Here I'm thinking of Hella Jongerius's 2019 project in Paris called *Interlace*, at Lafayette Anticipations. What makes this equipment so desirable for makers?

CM Well, first of all, I think it's great that she is experimenting with the digital Jacquard loom. I remember when she designed this textile series for Maharam, the *Repeat* series from 2002, and it was this large repeat. She shifted the scale for upholstery fabrics.... I mean, she dropped the mic! But I think the reason why other artists, including myself, are interested in hand-operated digital Jacquard looms—and there are others out there; AVL looms are in California, for example—is because they are extraordinarily flexible studio tools. I am an advocate for these looms. The only thing that you are constrained by is the width.

MO You tend to work in series—for instance, you began weaving the *Overshot* works in 2018—and today, you continue to use this structure. Does one weaving beget the next? Or is there a larger idea that you are working through, and therefore need several examples to articulate that broader idea?

CM Let me try to answer that by telling you a bit more about how I work. I will spend a full day in Photoshop mocking up the whole weaving because when I am working, I can only see a small segment of the textile. Because of these constraints, I can't spend a few weeks making something and then realize that the colors or textures don't work. In Photoshop, I will generate multiple versions while I'm working on one, which is why I tend to work in series. I think—I'm going to do this one first, but then, I'll go back to the other versions. Instead, I end up learning something instructive from the first weaving, and then when I go back to work on number two, I will try something new instead of going back to the original conception.

MO Do you ever think about cultural or artistic value? I was recently in Europe, where so many critics and curators were debating the value of design. I think with your work, this might be the place to introduce the idea of sustainability in your practice as another type of positive value.

CM I don't know. I care about textiles, whether there is an audience or not—and I believe that I will continue making them forever. Right now, I do this full-time because there is a venue for these works, but that could change tomorrow.

In terms of cultural value, I don't know. Making more stuff is a problem, but art, in general, has value in culture and in society. I think about my daughter in public school, and how the government is cutting arts funding. In fact, as a PTA, we are constantly fundraising to ensure that the humanities are part of education. It's just important—we need brilliant writers, thinkers, artists—and even more so today, when we are devaluing labor and human beings in general, which you can see in downtown L.A. every day.

I think in terms of the environment as another value, that we all have a responsibility as human

Fig. 13 Helen Frankenthaler, *Blue-Fall*, 1966. Acrylic on canvas, 89⅛ × 68¼ × 1⅜ in. Milwaukee Art Museum, Gift of Mrs. Henry Lynde Bradley

A Poem for Islands, 2016 (detail)

(Overleaf) *Fourwing Primrose Variation*, 2020 (detail)

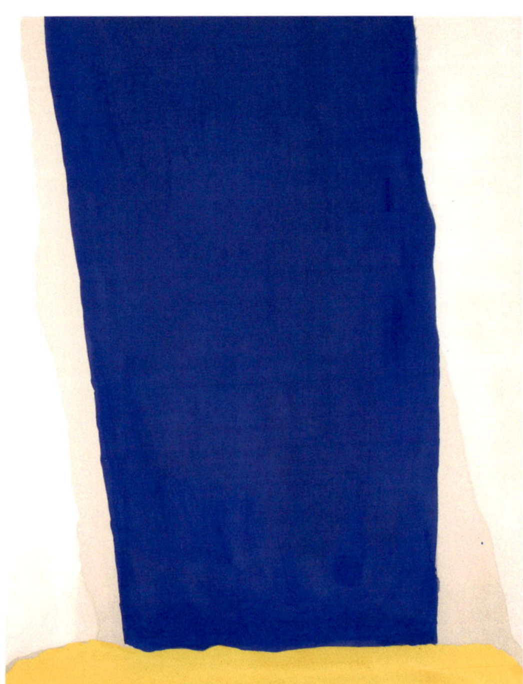

beings. I try to do as many things in my practice to have low impact, but I'm not kidding myself—when I use spray paint, that isn't good for the planet. My approach is, whenever possible, to use materials that were to be thrown out by an industrial company. In this way, they are diverting a small amount, but for my work, these discarded materials make up the bulk of my inventory. I really like to work with surplus and secondhand materials and then transform them into something else—a weaving that explores themes of landscape and geometry, or improvisation and atmosphere, for example.

MO Fun final question: Who are your art heroes?

CM Hands down, Helen Frankenthaler.... She is the first person that comes to mind. I love her experimental approach: the idea of pouring paint to create abstract canvases is inspiring (fig. 13). There is a looseness to her work, coupled with the way that she introduces color through chance, that is aspirational to me. My methodology is much more linear.

Of course, Anni Albers is also an incredible role model, and she is having a moment right now. I have a taped-together copy of *On Weaving* that I continue to reference. When I started teaching, I couldn't find any good scholarly readings, but Albers's *On Weaving* was it. Since then, I've been preaching the gospel of Anni Albers. What was inspiring about her practice was that she wasn't boxed into one type of making—she worked on an industrial scale, she made one-of-a-kind pieces, and then there was design work. Most importantly, she didn't distinguish one from the other. That was inspiring for me, coming out of school, because I had not really seen textile models: she was someone who was pursuing alternate avenues.

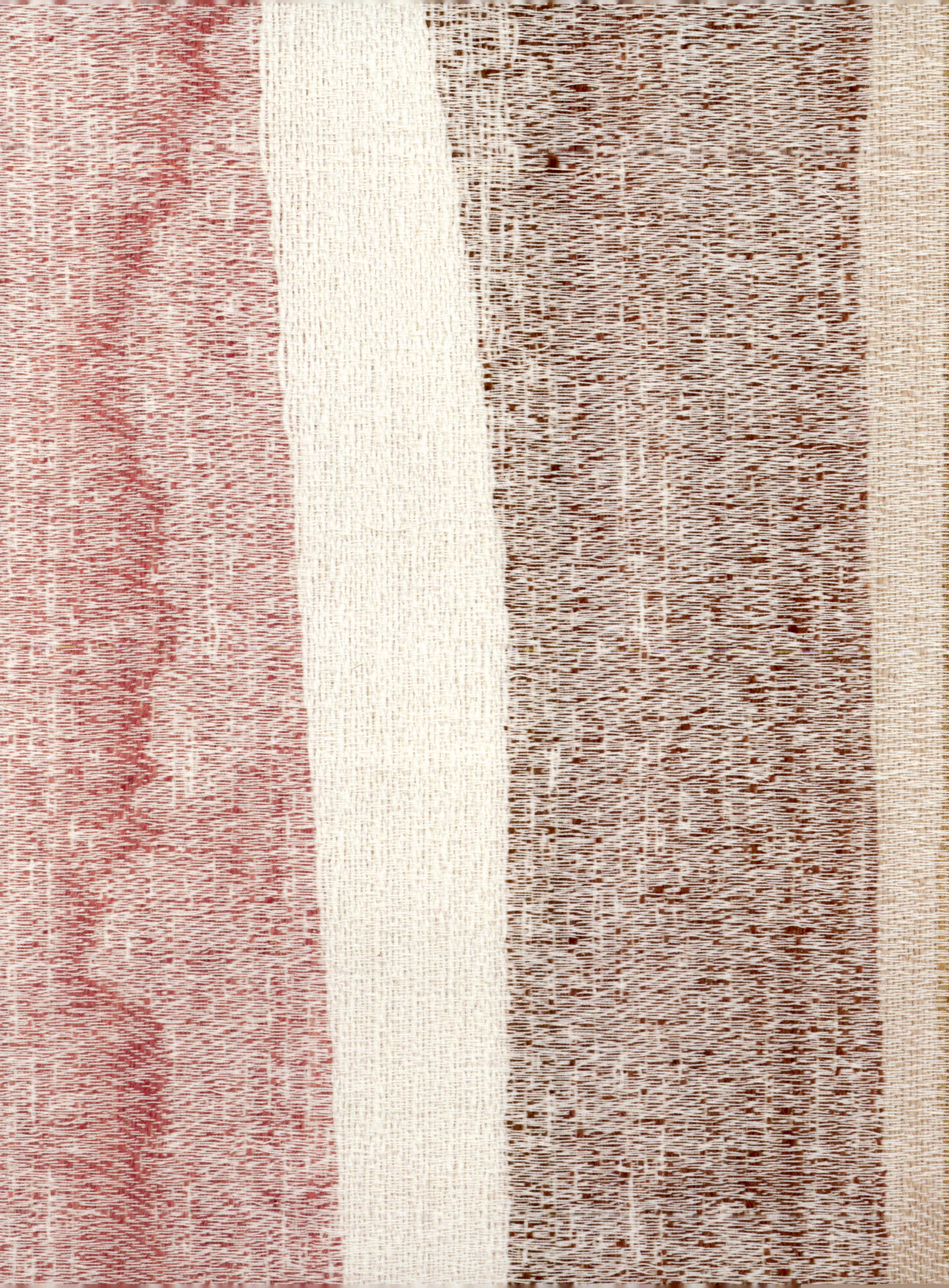

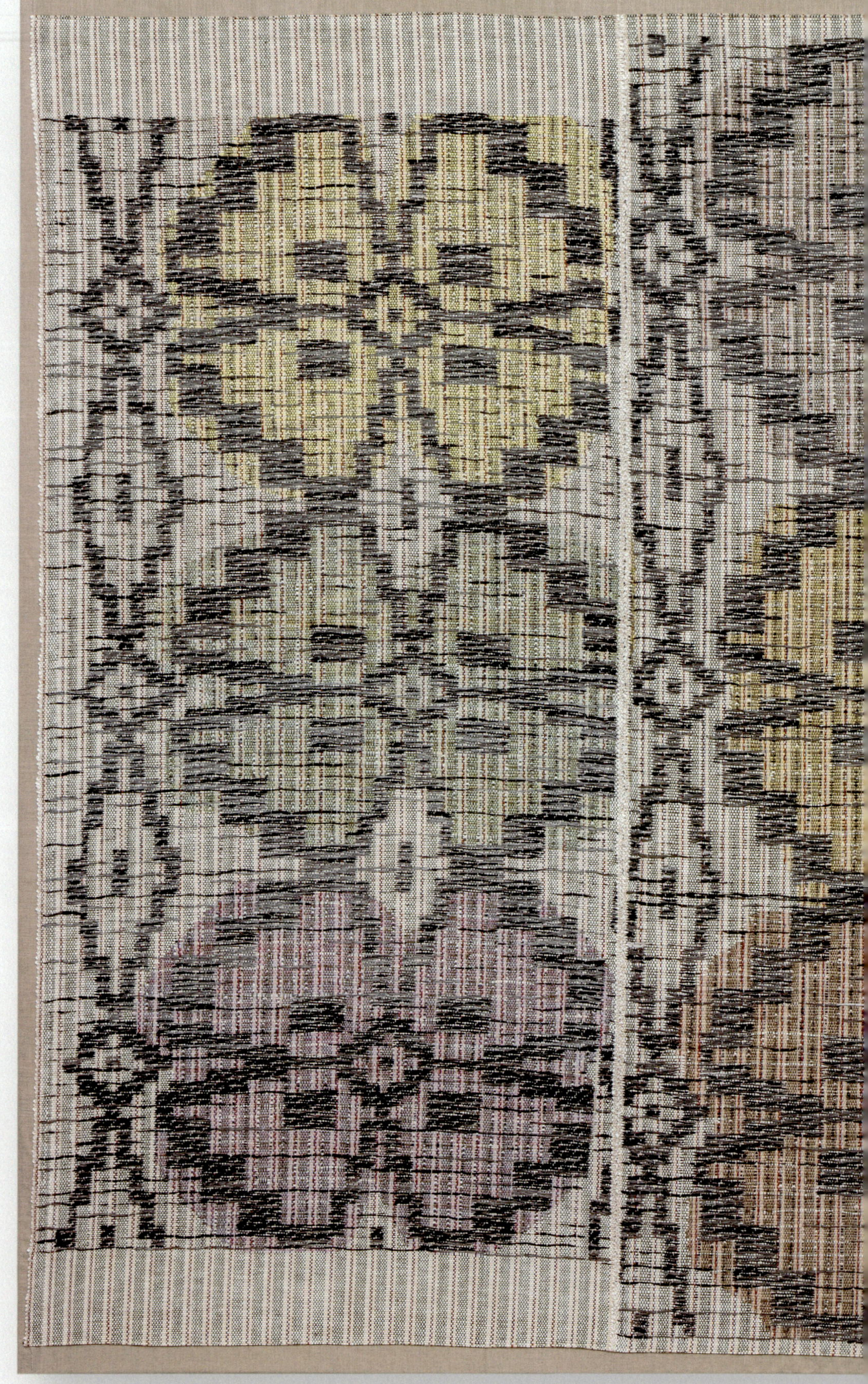

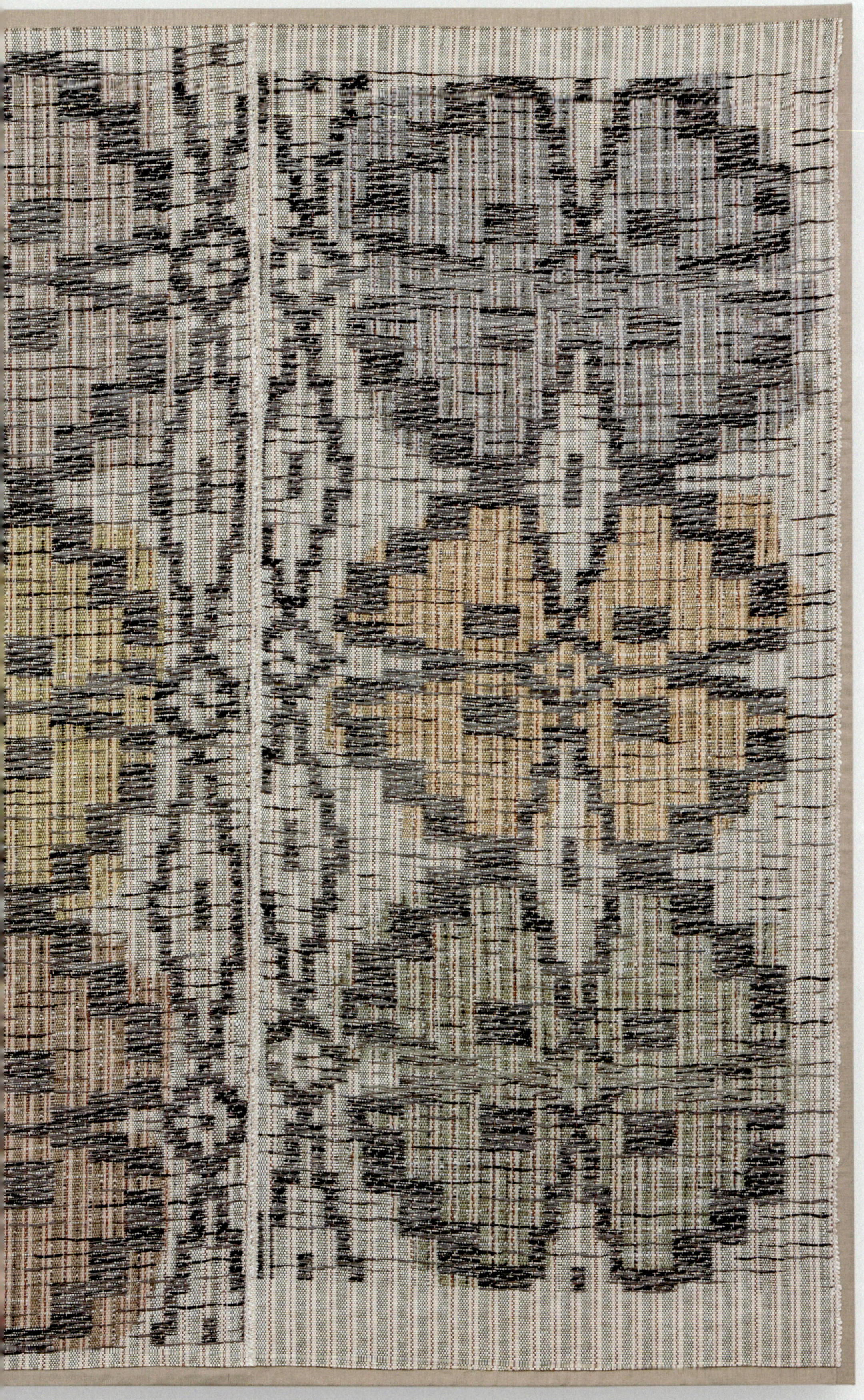

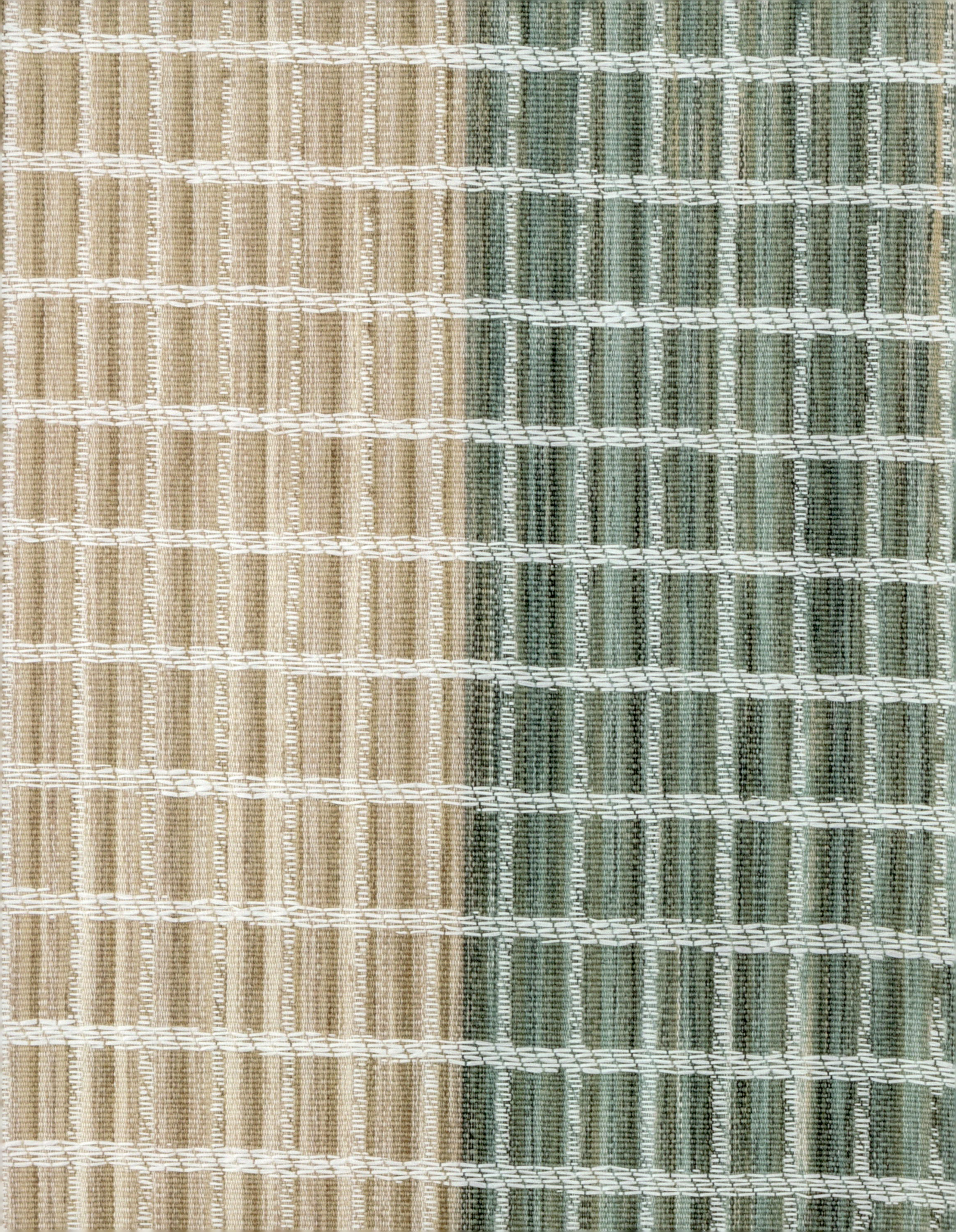

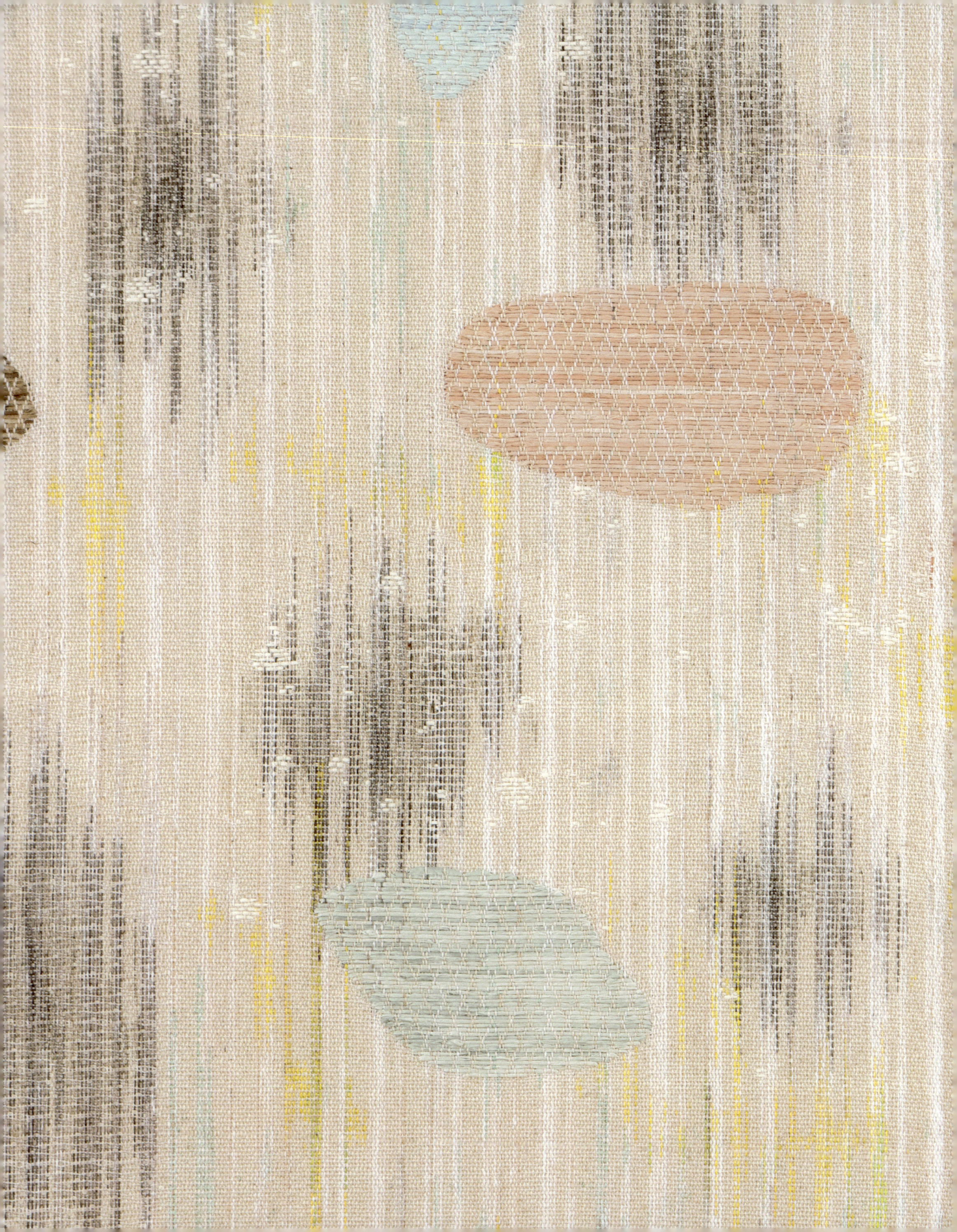

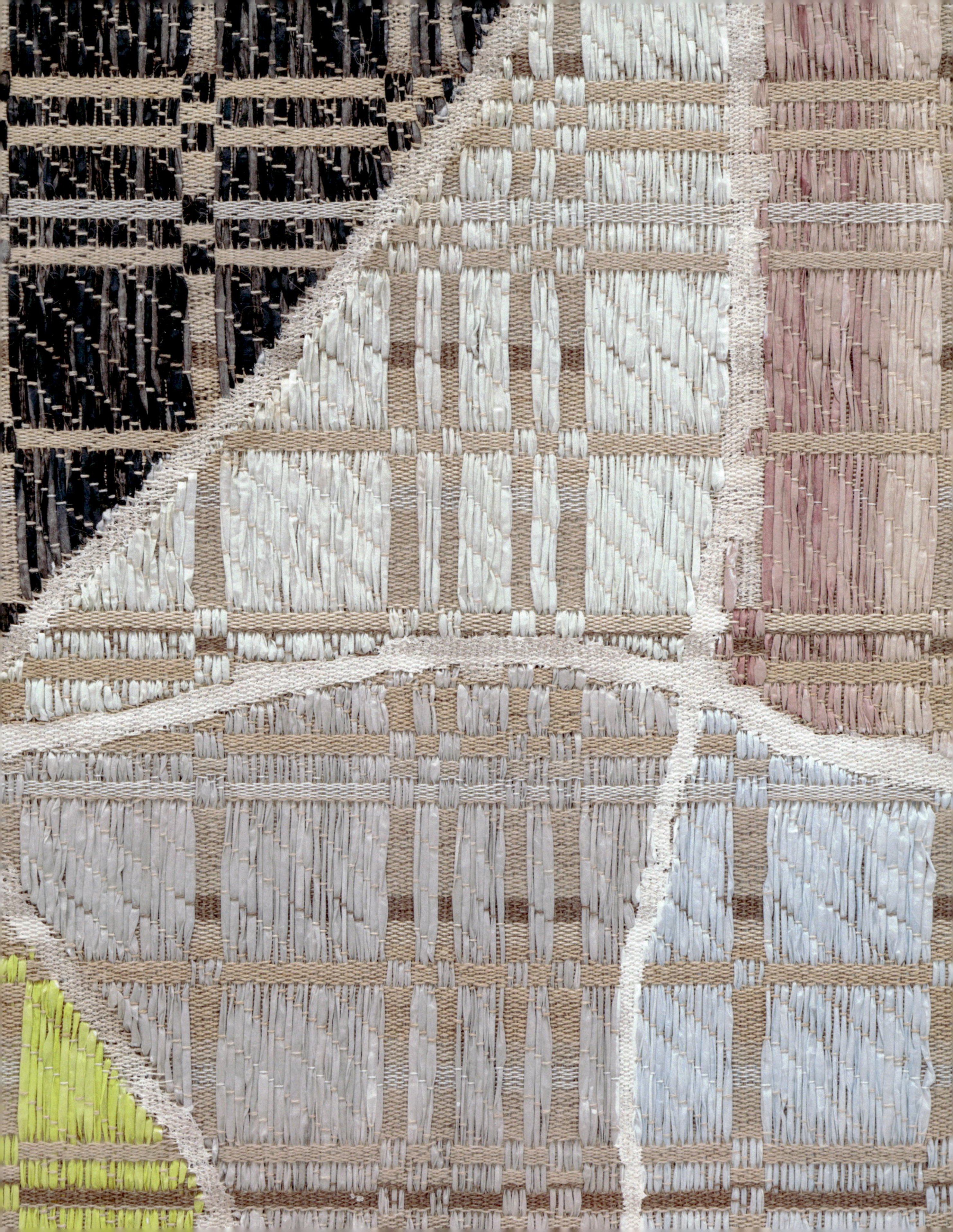

Exhibition Checklist

A Complete Thought, 2018
Cotton, wool, paper, spray paint, and acrylic
42½ × 42 in. (108 × 106.7 cm)
Private collection
(page 33)

A Poem for Islands, 2016
Cotton, wool, and natural dye
42½ × 66½ in. (108 × 168.9 cm)
Collection of Cecilia and Ira Wolfson
(page 69)

Buttonwillow, 2016
Alpaca, linen, cotton, and naturally dyed wool unique
25 × 22½ in. (63.5 × 57.2 cm)
Collection of Lizzy and Josh Scheinfeld

Change of Course (Twisted Grid), 2020
Acrylic, paper, and yarn
28½ × 20 in. (72.4 × 50.8 cm)
Courtesy of the artist and Rebecca Camacho Presents, San Francisco
(page 31)

Citrus, 2016
Alpaca, linen, cotton, and naturally dyed wool unique
25½ × 22¾ in. (64.8 × 57.8 cm)
Collection of Lizzy and Josh Scheinfeld

Disruption, 2018
Acrylic on paper, cotton, and linen
28 × 26 × 1½ in. (71.1 × 66 × 3.8 cm)
Collection of Teresa Manns
(page 20)

Double Bow Knot Variation, 2019
Acrylic and spray paint on paper, linen, naturally and commercially dyed cotton, and alpaca
29 × 24 in. (73.7 × 61 cm)
Courtesy of the artist and Volume Gallery, Chicago

Étoile, 2020
Acrylic, spray paint, and dye on paper and mixed fibers
39 × 58 in. (99.1 × 147.3 cm)
Collection of Lizzy and Josh Scheinfeld
(page 7)

Flowering Dogwood Variation, 2020
Acrylic, paper, linen, and wool
69 × 100 in. (175.3 × 254 cm)
Courtesy of the artist and Volume Gallery, Chicago
(page 48)

Fourwing Primrose Variation, 2020
Acrylic, paper, and linen
68½ × 99 in. (174 × 251.5 cm)
Courtesy of the artist and Volume Gallery, Chicago
(pages 70–71)

Full Moon Forest, 2016
Cotton, wool, and linen
46 × 43 in. (116.8 × 109.2 cm)
Collection of Monica Schaffer
(page 63)

Hershey, 2016
Alpaca, linen, cotton, and naturally dyed wool unique
25¾ × 22½ in. (65.4 × 57.2 cm)
Collection of Heiji and Brian Black
(page 14)

Horizontal Line, Variation II, 2019
Acrylic, spray paint, paper, linen, and wool
53 × 85½ in. (134.6 × 217.2 cm)
Courtesy of the artist and Volume Gallery, Chicago
(frontispiece)

I've Been Near You, but You've Never Noticed Me, 2016
Cotton, wool, and natural dye
42 × 57 in. (106.7 × 144.8 cm)
Art Institute of Chicago, Nicole Williams Contemporary Textile Fund, 2017.219
(page 8)

Love Is Like Seaweed, 2017
Paper, spray paint, alpaca, and linen
29 × 22 × 2 in. (73.7 × 55.9 × 5.1 cm)
Courtesy of the artist and Volume Gallery, Chicago

Magical Thinking, 2020
Acrylic, spray paint, and dye on paper and mixed fibers
62¼ × 87 in. (158.1 × 221 cm)
Milwaukee Art Museum, Purchase, with funds from Joel and Caran Quadracci and the Windhover Foundation
(pages 58–59, 78)

Many Horizons, 2020
Acrylic, paper, and yarn
37 × 57 in. (94 × 144.8 cm)
Courtesy of the artist and Rebecca Camacho Presents, San Francisco
(page 26)

Net, 2020
Acrylic, paper, and yarn
52 × 84½ in. (132.1 × 214.6 cm)
Courtesy of the artist and Rebecca Camacho Presents, San Francisco
(page 72)

Optics, 2018
Acrylic on paper, cotton, and linen
77 × 28 in. (195.6 × 71.1 cm)
Private collection
(page 19)

Optics II, 2018
Acrylic and spray paint on paper, cotton, and linen
52¼ × 43 in. (132.7 × 109.2 cm)
Courtesy of the artist and Volume Gallery, Chicago
(page 4)

Ouroboros, 2018
Acrylic and spray paint on paper, linen, cotton, and cashmere
43 × 28 in. (109.2 × 71.1 cm)
Courtesy of the artist and Volume Gallery, Chicago
(page 36)

Overshot Grid Variation, 2019
Acrylic on paper, deadstock linen, and wool
68 × 87 in. (172.7 × 221 cm)
Collection of McArthur Binion
(page 49)

Overshot Variation I, 2018
Acrylic and spray paint on Plotulopi, cotton, and wood
43¼ × 33¼ in. (109.9 × 84.5 cm)
Courtesy of the artist and Volume Gallery, Chicago
(pages 22, 40)

Overshot Variation II, 2018
Deadstock overspun linen, acrylic, and spray paint on paper, Einband Icelandic wool, cotton, and linen
43½ × 35¾ in. (110.5 × 90.8 cm)
Collection of Jennifer and Dan Gilbert
(page 41)

Overshot Variation 3, 2018
Acrylic and spray paint on Plotulopi, cotton, linen, alpaca, and cashmere on paper
33 × 58 in. (83.8 × 147.3 cm)
Los Angeles County Museum of Art, Gift of the 2019 Decorative Arts and Design Acquisition Committee (DA²), M.2019.245
(pages 42–43)

Overshot Variation 4, 2019/2020
Acrylic and spray paint on paper, linen, alpaca, cotton, and wool
34½ × 58½ in. (87.6 × 148.6 cm)
Collection of Gabrielle and Nick Sainati
(page 64)

Paragon, 2017
Paper, cotton, linen, wool, lopi, and alpaca
43 × 41 in. (109.2 × 104.1 cm)
Courtesy of the artist and Timothy Taylor Gallery, London and New York
(page 32)

Rose Knot Variation, 2020
Linen, paper thread painted with acrylic and spray paints, and wool
74 × 114 in. (188 × 289.6 cm)
Art Institute of Chicago, Textile Society Acquisition Fund, 2020.270

Rose Pattern Variation, 2019
Acrylic and spray paint on paper, linen, naturally and commercially dyed cotton, and alpaca
30 × 29¼ in. (76.2 × 74.3 cm)
Private collection

Stack, 2018
Acrylic on paper, cotton, and linen
41½ × 28 in. (105.4 × 71.1 cm)
Courtesy of the artist and Volume Gallery, Chicago
(page 21)

Synecdoche, 2018
Cotton, linen, paper, acrylic, and spray paint
39¼ × 29 in. (99.7 × 73.7 cm)
Private collection
(page 12)

Synecdoche II, 2018
Cotton, linen, paper, acrylic, and spray paint
39 × 29 in. (99.1 × 73.7 cm)
Private collection
(page 13)

Untitled (Always, Eventually), 2021
Acrylic and dye on paper and mixed fibers
44¼ × 56½ in. (112.4 × 143.5 cm)
Courtesy of the artist and Volume Gallery
(page 73)

Untitled (Clover), 2019
Fluid acrylic, paper, cotton, linen, and alpaca
21 × 20½ in. (53.3 × 52.1 cm)
Collection of McArthur Binion

Untitled (Flower Grid), 2021
Acrylic and indigo on paper, cotton, and alpaca
75½ × 86½ in. (191.8 × 219.7 cm)
Courtesy of the artist

Untitled (Grounds), 2019/2020
Fluid acrylic, paper, cotton, linen, and alpaca
29 × 33½ in. (73.7 × 85.1 cm)
Collection of McArthur Binion
(page 10)

Untitled (Kite), 2019
Fluid acrylic, spray paint, paper, cotton, linen, and alpaca
29½ × 26½ in. (74.9 × 67.3 cm)
Courtesy of the artist and Volume Gallery, Chicago
(page 74)

Untitled (Plots, reflected), 2019
Alpaca, linen, cotton, paper, spray paint, and acrylic
58½ × 51 in. (148.6 × 129.5 cm)
Courtesy of the artist and Volume Gallery, Chicago
(page 34)

Untitled (Reflection), 2017
Cotton, linen, paper, and acrylic on canvas
62 × 48 in. (157.48 × 121.92 cm)
Courtesy of the artist and Volume Gallery, Chicago

Untitled (Tabby), 2019
Acrylic, spray paint, linen, cotton, alpaca, and wool
28½ × 17½ in. (72.4 × 44.5 cm)
Courtesy of the artist and Timothy Taylor Gallery, London and New York
(page 66)

Untitled (Turbine), 2018
Acrylic and spray paint on paper, linen, and cotton
28 × 32 in. (71.1 × 81.3 cm)
Courtesy of the artist and Volume Gallery, Chicago
(page 30)

Untitled (Winding I), 2019
Acrylic, spray paint, natural dye, paper, cotton, linen, and alpaca
48½ × 85 in. (123.2 × 215.9 cm)
Collection of Kelly Padden and Mathias Kessler
(page 52)

Untitled (Winding II), 2019
Acrylic, spray paint, natural dye, paper, cotton, linen, and alpaca
52 × 85 in. (132.1 × 215.9 cm)
Courtesy of the artist and Volume Gallery, Chicago
(page 53)

Untitled (Window), 2021
Acrylic and dye on paper and mixed fibers
24¾ × 24¾ in. (62.9 × 62.9 cm)
Courtesy of the artist and Volume Gallery, Chicago

Wattle, 2016
Alpaca, linen, cotton, and naturally dyed wool unique
25 × 22¼ in. (63.5 × 56.5 cm)
Collection of Lisa and Philip Kepler
(page 50)

Wyo, 2016
Alpaca, linen, cotton, and naturally dyed wool unique
25 × 22½ in. (63.5 × 57.2 cm)
Collection of Margo Wolowiec
(page 51)

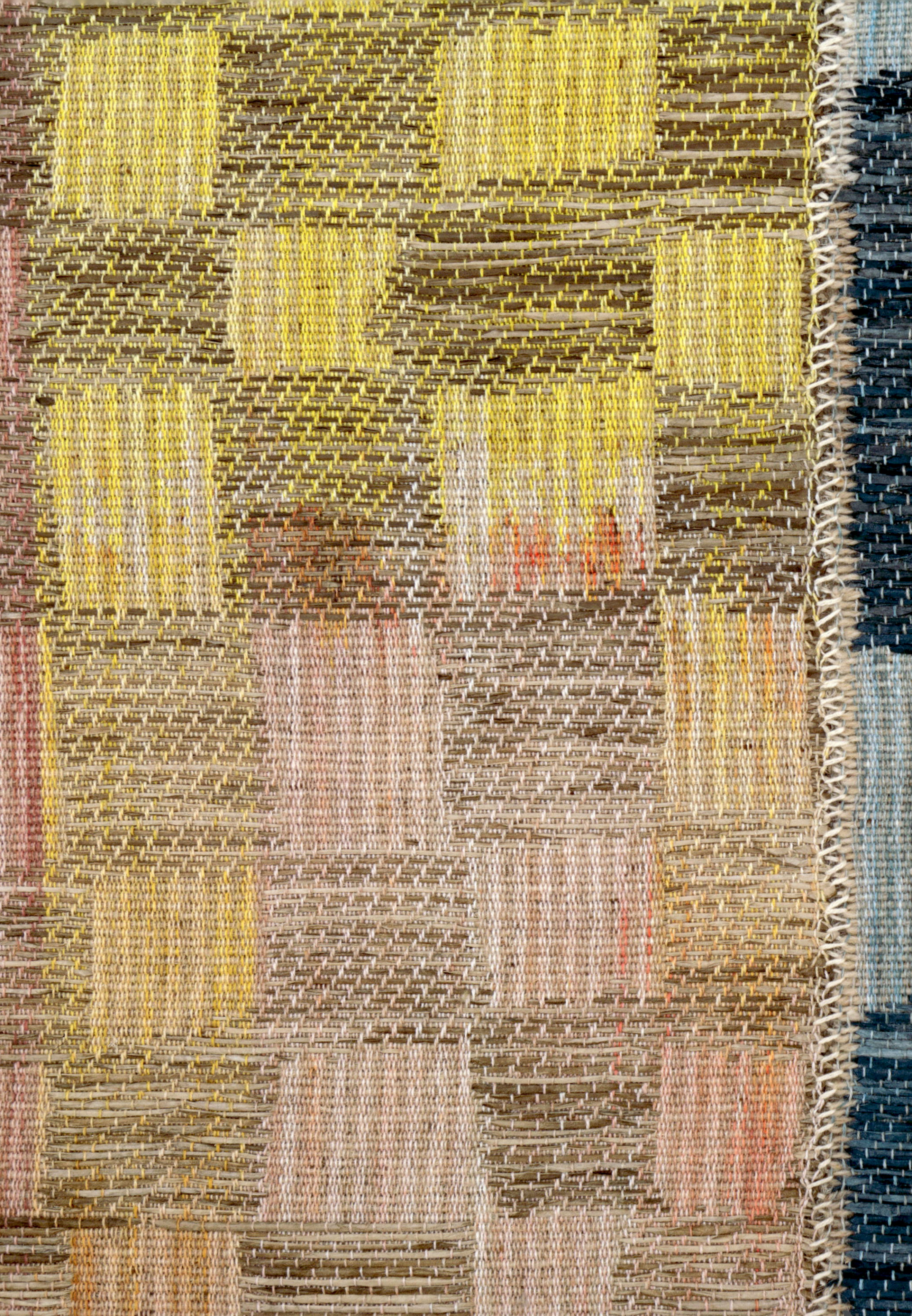

Contributors

Monica Obniski is Curator of Decorative Arts and Design at the High Museum of Art, Atlanta. She formerly served as the Demmer Curator of 20th- and 21st-Century Design at the Milwaukee Art Museum.

Marcelle Polednik, PhD, is the Donna and Donald Baumgartner Director of the Milwaukee Art Museum.

Su Wu is a writer and curator based in Mexico City.

Library of Congress Control Number:
2021942209
ISBN 978-1-64657-019-5

Published by the Milwaukee Art Museum
700 North Art Museum Drive
Milwaukee, Wisconsin 53202
www.mam.org

Available through ARTBOOK | D.A.P.
75 Broad Street, Suite 630, New York, NY 10004
www.artbook.com

This research was supported by a Craft Research Fund grant from the Center for Craft, Asheville, North Carolina.

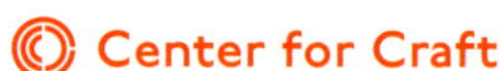

Produced by Lucia | Marquand, Seattle
www.luciamarquand.com
Edited by Tanya Heinrich
Designed by Ryan Polich
Typeset in Söhne by Tina Henderson
Proofread by Brynn Warriner
Color management by iocolor, Seattle
Printed and bound in China by Artron Art Group

Detail images:
Frontispiece: *Horizontal Line, Variation II*, 2019
Page 4: *Optics II*, 2018
Page 7: *Étoile*, 2020
Page 8: *I've Been Near You, but You've Never Noticed Me*, 2016
Page 10: *Untitled (Grounds)*, 2019/2020
Page 34: *Untitled (Plots, reflected)*, 2019
Page 72: *Net*, 2020
Page 73: *Untitled (Always, Eventually)*, 2021
Page 74: *Untitled (Kite)*, 2019
Page 78: *Magical Thinking*, 2020

Photography:
Frontispiece, pages 10, 26, 31–32, 34, 48, 52–53, 64, 66, 70–72, 74: Joshua White, Los Angeles. Pages 4, 7–8, 12–15, 19–22, 24–25, 30, 33, 36, 40–41, 46, 49–51, 58–59, 63, 69, 73, 78: Volume Gallery, Chicago. Page 16, left: © 2020 The Josef and Anni Albers Foundation / Artists Rights Society (ARS), New York. Pages 16, right, and 17: John R. Glembin. Page 23: © The Art Institute of Chicago / Art Resource, NY. Page 37: © 2020 Dorothea Rockburne / Artists Rights Society (ARS), New York / Light Blue Studio. Pages 42–43: Los Angeles County Museum of Art, © 2021, Museum Associates / LACMA. Licensed by Art Resource, NY. Page 44: © 2002 Nicholas Gessler. Page 54: Molly Haas. Page 68: Efraim Lev-er, © 2010 Helen Frankenthaler / Artists Rights Society (ARS), New York.

Published on the occasion of *Currents 38: Christy Matson*, on view February 25–July 17, 2022.

Since its founding in 1888, the Milwaukee Art Museum has been committed to exhibiting and collecting the art of its time. The Museum presents a variety of exhibitions, programs, and publications designed to introduce its visitors to the work of contemporary artists. Initiated in 1982, the *Currents* exhibition series brings significant work by living artists into the Museum. Through these exhibitions, the Museum has made key acquisitions that are now cornerstones of its contemporary collection.

Currents Series

1982 Currents 1: Cynthia Carlson
1982 Currents 2: New Figuration from Europe
1983 Currents 3: Richard DeVore
1983 Currents 4: Art and Use
1984 Currents 5: Video Installations
1984 Currents 6: New Abstraction
1985 Currents 7: Words in Action
1985 Currents 8: Robert Turner: A Potter's Retrospective
1986 Currents 9: Various
1987 Currents 10: Julian Schnabel
1987 Currents 11: Mülheimer Freiheit Group
1987 Currents 12: Simulations: New American Conceptualism
1988 Currents 13: Francesco Clemente: The Graphic Work
1989 Currents 14: Ross Bleckner
1989 Currents 15: Various
1989 Currents 16: Terry Winters: Drawings
1990 Currents 17: Meg Webster
1991 Currents 18: Cindy Sherman: The Masters Series
1991 Currents 19: Eric Fischloff: Drawings
1992 Currents 20: Recent Narrative Sculpture
1992 Currents 21: Louise Bourgeois
1993 Currents 22: Felix Gonzalez-Torres
1994 Currents 23: Damien Hirst
1994 Currents 24: Stan Douglas
1995 Currents 25: Kiki Smith: Prints and Multiples, 1985–1993
1997 Currents 26: Ed Ruscha
1998 Currents 27: Andreas Gursky
2000 Currents 28: Hiroshi Sugimoto
2001 Currents 29: Rodney Graham
2002 Currents 30: Rachel Harrison
2004 Currents 31: Robert Melee
2006 Currents 32: Gord Peteran
2007 Currents 33: Gregor Schneider
2012 Currents 34: Isaac Julien "Expeditions"
2012 Currents 35: Tara Donovan
2013 Currents 36: Dirk Skreber
2017 Currents 37: LAWRENCE WEINER: INHERENT INNATE TENSION
2022 Currents 38: Christy Matson